LONGMAN
CORNERSTONE

PHONICS
and Word Analysis

PEARSON
Longman

**Longman Cornerstone
Phonics and Word Analysis**

Copyright © by Pearson Education, Inc.

Pearson Education, 10 Bank Street, White Plains, NY 10606

Staff credits: The people who made up the *Longman Cornerstone Phonics and Word Analysis* team, representing editorial, production, design, manufacturing, and marketing, are John Ade, Rhea Banker, Liz Barker, Kenna Bourke, Jeffrey Buckner, Brandon Carda, Daniel Comstock, Martina Deignan, Gina DiLillo, Nancy Flaggman, Cate Foley, Patrice Fraccio, Tracy Grenier, Zach Halper, Henry Hild, Sarah Hughes, Karen Kawaguchi, Lucille M. Kennedy, Ed Lamprich, Jamie Lawrence, Niki Lee, Christopher Leonowicz, Tara Maceyak, Katrinka Moore, Linda Moser, Liza Pleva, Edie Pullman, Monica Rodriguez, Tara Rose, Tania Saiz-Sousa, Chris Siley, Heather St. Clair, Loretta Steves, and Andrew Vaccaro.
Text design and composition: TSI Graphics
Photo credit: shutterstock.com

ISBN-13: 978-0-13-813662-8
ISBN-10: 0-13-813662-9

PEARSON LONGMAN ON THE **WEB**

Pearsonlongman.com offers online resources for teachers and students. Access our Companion Websites, our online catalog, and our local offices around the world.

Visit us at **www.pearsonlongman.com.**

Printed in the United States of America
8 9 10— VOLL —12 11

CONTENTS

Name _____ Date _____

Alphabet Review

A. Say the letters of the alphabet out loud. Point to each letter as you read it.

Aa	Bb	Cc	Dd	Ee
Ff	Gg	Hh	Ii	Jj
Kk	Ll	Mm	Nn	Oo
Pp	Qq	Rr	Ss	Tt
Uu	Vv	Ww	Xx	Yy
Zz				

B. Read the letters out loud with a partner.

Alphabet Review

A. Each letter of the alphabet has an uppercase letter and a lowercase letter. Name each uppercase letter. Circle its matching lowercase letter.

1. C   a   y   c

2. P   p   j   k

3. T   m   o   t

4. E   e   l   x

5. Z   u   d   z

6. F   b   f   w

7. S   n   s   g

8. H   h   i   q

B. Name each lowercase letter. Circle its matching uppercase letter.

1. r   V   R   M

2. a   A   M   C

3. j   Q   J   S

4. b   D   R   B

5. k   K   O   Y

6. l   X   F   L

7. e   E   I   U

8. p   C   P   J

Name _____   Date _____

Consonant Sound-Spelling Review

> These letters are consonants: *b, c, d, f, g, h, j, k, l, m, n, p, q, r, s, t, v, w, x, y, z.*

A. Say each consonant letter name out loud. Review the sound each consonant makes.

B. Look at each picture. Say its name out loud. Circle the letter that the picture name begins with.

1.

d   b   c

2.

j   c   t

3.

k   n   s

4.

p   s   w

5.

t   h   j

C. Draw a picture of an object that begins with *b, c, k, s,* or *t.*

Name _____ Date _____

Consonant Sound-Spelling Review

These letters are consonants: *b, c, d, f, g, h, j, k, l, m, n, p, q, r, s, t, v, w, x, y, z.* Review the sound each consonant makes.

A. Look at each picture. Say its name out loud. Draw a line from each picture to the letter that stands for its beginning sound.

1.   G

2.   V

3.   R

4.   L

5.   P

B. Draw a picture of a food that begins with *g, l, p, r,* or *v.*

Name _____ Date _____

Consonant Sound-Spelling Review

These letters are consonants: *b, c, d, f, g, h, j, k, l, m, n, p, q, r, s, t, v, w, x, y, z*. Review the sound each consonant makes.

A. Look at each picture. Say its name out loud. Write the letter that the picture name begins with.

1. _____

2. _____

3. _____

4. _____

5. _____

B. Draw a picture of an animal that begins with *f, h, j, w,* or *z*.

Consonant Sound-Spelling Review

These letters are consonants: *b, c, d, f, g, h, j, k, l, m, n, p, q, r, s, t, v, w, x, y, z*. Review the sound each consonant makes. *X* and *q* are special consonants. *Q* is always next to *u*. *Qu* makes the /kw/ sound. *X* usually comes at the end of a word and says /ks/.

A. Look at each picture. Say its name out loud. Circle the letter that the picture name begins or ends with.

1.	**2.**	**3.**
n t m	d f x	j t s
4.	**5.**	**6.**
qu l r	b v n	t x n

B. Draw a picture of an object that begins with *d, m, n, t, qu,* or *y*.

Short Vowels

Name _____ Date _____

Short *a*

Sometimes the *a* sound is at the beginning of words.

A. Look at the pictures. Say the words out loud.

1.

apple

2.

ant

3.

alligator

4.

anchor

B. Draw a line to match the words.

1. can   an

2. am   had

3. an   at

4. at   can

5. had   am

Name _____ Date _____

Short *a*

> Sometimes the *a* sound is in the middle of words.

A. Look at the pictures. Say the words out loud.

1.

bat

2.

cab

3.

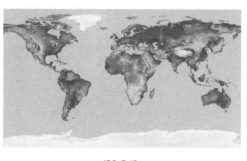

map

4.

fan

B. Read the sentences out loud. Circle the words with short *a* sound.

1. I am a cat.

2. A cat had a can.

3. I had a cat.

4. I ran.

5. I am Dad.

High Frequency Words: Set 1

A. You will see these 10 words in many books. Say the words out loud.

that	the	is	you	to
me	are	see	what	like

B. Read these sentences out loud. Circle the high frequency words.

1. What is that?

2. That is a cat.

3. I like the cat.

4. The cat can see me.

5. The cat ran to me.

6. Are you Pam?

7. Are you Sam?

8. I see that you are Pat.

9. What is it?

10. You ran to me.

Reading Practice: Passage 1

A. Read the story out loud.

I see a hat.
I see a cat.
I see a bat.
I see a pan.

What is that?
That is a can.
Can I see the can?
I like the can.

B. Work with a partner. Answer each question.

1. What can I see?

2. What did I like?

Home-School Connection Read the story to a family member or a friend. Ask him or her to read it again with you.

Chapter 1: Short Vowels 11

Short *i*

> Sometimes the *i* sound is at the beginning of words.

A. Look at the pictures. Say the words out loud.

1.

igloo

2.

iguana

3.

insect

B. Write the letter *i*. Then read the words out loud.

1. _____s

2. _____t

3. _____n

4. _____f

C. Choose a word from the box to complete each sentence.

in   is   it

1. I like _____.

2. A cat is _____ that can.

3. What _____ that?

Name _____   Date _____

Short *i*

> Sometimes the *i* sound is in the middle of words.

A. Look at the pictures. Say the words out loud.

1.

sit

2.

mitt

B. Read the sentences out loud. Circle the words with short *i* sound.

1.   Tim has six big cats.

2.   I hid the tin can.

3.   Can Jim sit?

C. Read the words in the box. Underline words with short *i* sound. Circle words with short *a* sound.

big	it	at	is
cat	pin	had	him
man	ran	jam	did
pig	if	am	six

Short *o*

> Sometimes the *o* sound is at the beginning of words.

A. Look at the pictures. Say the words out loud.

1.

ox

2.

octopus

B. Write the letter *o*. Then read the words out loud.

1. d____t

2. j____g

3. t____p

4. m____p

5. f____g

6. h____t

C. Circle the word that completes each sentence. Read the sentences.

1. What is on the (tap, top) of the hat?

2. Did Tim (jog, jig) to the top?

3. The cat is (hot, hip).

4. The hog is on the (pat, log).

5. I like to see (fog, lap).

Name _____ Date _____

Short *o*

> Sometimes the *o* sound is in the middle of words.

A. Look at the pictures. Say the words out loud.

1.

box

2.

fox

B. Choose a word from the box to complete each sentence.

pot   top   fox

1. The _____ ran.

2. What is in that hot _____?

3. A _____ is on the box.

◎ **C. Read the sentences out loud. Fill in the chart with the *a, i,* and *o* words.**

It is hot.   Jim is not hot.
Jim ran to a box.   Pam is not hot.
Pam the fox hid in the big can.

a	*i*	*o*

Consonant *s*

> Sometimes the letter *s* can make the *z* sound.

A. Read the words with the *z* sound out loud. Circle the letter *s* in each word.

1. has   **2.** is   **3.** as   **4.** his

B. Read the words in the box out loud. Circle them in the word find.

is	as	his	was	has

w	z	a	i	h
w	h	a	s	o
a	i	s	z	w
s	s	h	o	s
i	h	a	z	s

C. Complete each sentence with a word from the box above.

1. Sam _____ a big dog.

2. _____ dog is on the bag.

3. That dog is _____ big _____ my dog.

4. What _____ that dog like?

Name _____   Date _____

Nouns with -s

Sometimes the letter *s* is added to words. When *s* is added to a singular noun, it makes it plural, or more than one.

A. Read the words out loud.

Nouns with -s	
hats	ants
pigs	cats
cans	bats

B. Read the words out loud. Circle the -s words.

1. cat   cats   cot

2. pots   pot   pat

3. mop   tin   mops

4. lip   ham   lips

5. hot   hats   ant

C. Complete each sentence with the correct form of the word. Read the sentences out loud.

1. (cat) Tom has six _____.

2. (rat) Did you see the _____?

3. (pin) Kim has the _____.

4. (pot) Please wash the _____.

Final Double Consonants

Sometimes a word will end with two consonants that are the same. We call these two letters *double consonants*. A double consonant stands for one sound.

A. Read the words with double final consonants out loud.

1. off   **2.** will   **3.** miss   **4.** doll

B. Read the sentences out loud. Circle words that have a double consonant.

1. Miss Pam has six cans.

2. Pick the top off the can.

3. Did Mom kiss you?

4. Bill is the boss.

5. Dad will drive the car.

C. Add *ll*, *ff*, or *ss* to complete the words. Then read the words out loud.

1. mi _____, mi _____

2. to _____

3. o _____

4. do _____

5. hi _____, hi _____

6. wi _____

Name _____ Date _____

Short *e*

Sometimes the e sound is at the beginning of words.

A. Look at the pictures. Say the words out loud.

1.

egg

2.

elephant

B. Read the sentences out loud. Underline the words with short e sound.

1.   The red hen has ten eggs.

2.   Jen tells him to sit.

3.   I see a mess on the bed.

4.   Tell Ben to get well.

5.   Yes, I let the cat in.

C. Answer each riddle with a word from the box.

bed   hen

1.   I am red.
I sit on eggs.
What am I?

_____

2.   I am big.
You can nap on me.
What am I?

_____

Short *e*

Sometimes the *e* sound is in the middle of words.

A. Look at the pictures. Say the words out loud.

1.

bed

2.

tell

B. Underline the *e* sound in each word. Then write a word that rhymes next to it.

1. hen   _____

2. bed   _____

3. let   _____

4. peg   _____

◎ **C.** Complete words by writing *a, i, o,* or *e* in the blanks.

1. p____n, d____n, t____n, h____n

2. b____d, r____d, f____d, m____d

3. l____t, p____t, s____t, d____t

4. b____g, w____g, r____g, t____g

5. t____p, p____p, m____p, l____p

High Frequency Words: Set 2

A. You will see these 10 words in many books. Say the words out loud.

and	for	look	make	one
does	he	she	your	of

B. Read these sentences out loud. Circle the high frequency words.

1. Look at this big bag of pets.

2. He likes to make bells.

3. I make pets for mom and dad.

4. I can make jam for your mom and dad.

5. What does your mom like?

6. That one sits on the top.

7. She is red.

8. Will you make it for me?

9. He is big.

10. Look at the pig.

11. She has a hat.

12. That one is fat.

Reading Practice: Passage 2

A. Read the story out loud.

What can you make?
I can make jam.
I can make ham.
I can make eggs.

I pick six eggs.
I can make eggs well.
I mix the eggs.
I get a pan.
I let the eggs sit.
Look! The eggs are hot. Mmmm.

B. Work with a partner. Answer each question.

1. Does the story tell how to make ham or eggs?

2. How many eggs did she pick?

Home-School Connection Read the story to a family member or a friend. Ask that person to tell you their favorite breakfast meal. Does he or she like eggs?

Name _____ Date _____

Short *u*

Sometimes the *u* sound is at the beginning of words.

A. Look at the pictures. Say the words out loud.

1.

up

2.

umbrella

B. Read the sentences out loud. Underline words with short *u* sound.

1. I like to hug the dog.

2. The cup is red.

3. Look at the bug run!

4. The wet cub is in a tub.

5. A duck can quack

C. Draw a line to show words that rhyme.

1. bun   tub
2. rub   fun
3. luck   rug
4. cup   tuck
5. dug   pup

Name _____   Date _____

Short *u*

Sometimes the *u* sound is in the middle of words.

A. Look at the pictures. Say the words out loud.

1.

duck

2.

sun

B. Circle the words with *u* sound. Read the sentences out loud.

1. She fell in the mud.

2. The mug is hot.

3. One bug is on that hat.

C. Read the story out loud. Fill in the chart below with the *a, e, i, o, u* words.

Pup is a fox. He can lick. He can run. He can dig in the mud. Pup is fun in the tub. Pup can hug. He is a fun pet!

a	e	i	o	u

Possessives with 's

Some words end with an apostrophe and the letter *s*.
An *'s* shows ownership of something.

A. Read the examples in the box out loud.

Noun	Possessive
Pam Jim hen Pat	Pam's Jim's hen's Pat's

B. Add 's to each word. Then say the words out loud.

1. Tom_____

2. Tim_____

3. cat_____

4. Sam_____

C. Read the sentences out loud. Underline the words with 's.
   Circle what the person owns.

1. Todd's hat fell off.

2. Look for Jen's ten cans.

3. Ben's dog is big.

4. Does Kim's pup like to run?

5. Tim's cap fell in the well.

6. I like Pam's book.

CVC Syllables: Phonograms

Many words have the consonant-vowel-consonant or CVC syllable pattern. CVC words often are phonograms. Phonograms are one-syllable words that can be grouped by word families.

A. Read the words out loud. Write the words into the correct word families.

rat	mat	led	sat	jot	tin	fin	up	tot	win
bed	cot	red	pin	pup	cup	Ted	cat	sup	not

-at	-ot	-ed	-up	-in

B. Read the words out loud. Write another word that is in the same word family.

1. rip _____

2. mug _____

3. tap _____

4. nod _____

5. bet _____

Chapter 1 Review

A. Complete the sentences by adding -s or a possessive 's to the words. Read the sentences out loud.

1. (Pam) _____ cat is on the bed.

2. I see the (pan) _____ on top.

3. Look for (Jim) _____ hat.

4. He has (pin) _____ in that cup.

5. (Mom) _____ leg got cut.

6. Jan has the red (pen) _____.

7. (Jeff) _____ cup is big.

8. Does Jess like (egg) _____?

9. Tell the (kid) _____ to run.

B. Read the story out loud. Fix the spelling of the underlined words.

We like pets. Cal has a cat. His <u>cot</u> _____ likes to nap.
            10

Peg has a <u>dig</u> _____. Peg's dog can <u>sat</u> _____
     11   12

and run. Jack has a <u>pog</u> _____. That pig is <u>beg</u>
         13   14

_____! What is your <u>pat</u> _____?
                         15

Chapter 1 Review (continued)

C. Read the words out loud. Write a rhyming word.

16. tin   win   _____

17. pick   sick   _____

18. bell   well   _____

19. cut   but   _____

20. tag   wag   _____

21. pot   cot   _____

22. bun   sun   _____

23. lab   dab   _____

24. sat   mat   _____

D. Read the words out loud. Circle each word in the word find.

will	off	his	well	yes

w	y	a	h	i	s	s
w	e	o	f	a	f	f
i	s	s	w	e	l	l
l	s	l	o	f	f	s
l	y	h	a	m	s	s

Consonant Blends and Digraphs

Initial Blends: *sp*, *st*, *sm*

In a consonant blend, two or three consonants appear together. Each consonant sound is pronounced.

A. Look at the pictures. Say the words out loud. Circle the initial blend sounds.

1.  spill	**2.**  stop	**3.**  smash
4.  spell	**5.**  step	**6.**  small

B. Read the words out loud. Circle the words that begin with *sp*, *st*, and *sm*.

1. sick   spell   sock

2. son   sip   stop

3. smack   silly   sock

4. step   sell   sand

5. sun   smash   Sam

6. sat   sit   still

Name _____ Date _____

Initial Blends: *sl, sw, sn, sk*

> Remember that in a consonant blend, each consonant sound is pronounced.

A. Look at the pictures. Say the words out loud. Circle the initial blend sounds.

1.

sled

2.

swim

3.

snack

4.

sky

B. Read the words out loud. Write a rhyming word that begins with *sw, sn, sk,* or *sl.*

1. bed   _____

2. dim   _____

3. tap   _____

4. lip   _____

5. kid   _____

Initial Blends: *tr, br, gr*

Remember that in a consonant blend, each consonant sound is pronounced.

A. Look at the pictures. Say the words out loud. Circle the initial blend sounds.

1.	2.	3.
track	brick	grin
4.	**5.**	**6.**
tractor	broccoli	grapes

B. Read the words out loud. Circle each word in the word find.

grin	grab	brick	brag	trim	trip

a	g	r	i	n	b
b	r	r	b	b	r
r	d	t	a	e	i
a	f	r	r	b	c
g	g	i	h	i	k
n	i	m	k	l	p

Name _____ Date _____

Initial Blends: *fr*, *cr*, *pr*

Remember that in a consonant blend, each consonant sound is pronounced.

A. Look at the pictures. Say the words out loud. Circle the initial blend sounds.

1.  frog	2.  crab	3.  present
4.  fruit	5.  crayon	6. prince

B. Read the words out loud. Circle the two words that have the same initial blend.

1. crack   rack   crop

2. pretty   package   print

3. cross   cram   cot

4. freeze   fog   Fran

5. crisp   cat   crab

6. fruit   free   fan

High Frequency Words: Set 3

A. You will see these 10 words in many books. Say the words out loud.

come find down here from said where we do they

B. Read these sentences out loud. Circle the high frequency words.

1. Spot the dog can not find his pal, Tim.

2. "Where is Tim?" said Spot.

3. "Come down here," said Fred.

4. "We can run up and down the hill to look for Tim," he said.

5. Spot said, "I do not like to run up from down here."

6. "Where is he? What can we do?" said Spot.

7. "Come here," said Kim and Bill.

8. They can swim to find him.

9. Spot said, "I do not like to get wet."

10. "Can you find Tim for me?"

11. They swam to look for his pal, Tim.

12. "We see Tim down here," they said.

13. "Where did you come from?" said Tim.

14. "We are here to find you," they said.

Name _____ Date _____

Reading Practice: Passage 3

A. Read the story out loud.

Stan had a red sled. He got the sled from his mom. Stan's sled slid down the big hill. It slid down the steps. The sled hit a pile of sticks. Stan fell off the sled and bumped his leg. Stan did not see his sled. He had to try and find it.

B. Work with a partner. Answer each question.

1. Where did Stan's sled go?

2. What did Stan's sled hit?

Home-School Connection Read the story to a family member or a friend. Discuss how to be safe when sledding. Do you think Stan was careful?

Initial Blends: *cl, bl, gl*

> Remember that in a consonant blend, each consonant sound is pronounced.

A. Look at the pictures. Say the words out loud. Circle the initial blend sounds.

1.	2.	3.

clock	block	glass
4.	5.	6.

clam	blanket	glue

B. Add *cl, bl,* or *gl* to finish the words. Read the words out loud.

1. _____ap

2. _____ack

3. _____ip

4. _____ad

5. _____ock

6. _____ue

Initial Blends: *fl*, *pl*

> Remember that in a consonant blend, each consonant sound is pronounced.

A. Look at the pictures. Say the words out loud. Circle the initial blend sounds.

1.  flag	**2.**  flip	**3.**  plug
4.  flamingo	**5.**  Pluto	**6.**  plant

B. Read the words out loud. Circle the words with initial blends *fl* and *pl*.

1. flat   plan   fat   flop

2. plot   put   plop   pop

3. fan   flip   flap   plug

4. fun   flute   food   flu

5. plum   Pam   play   pot

Name _____ Date _____

Final Blends: *nt, nd*

Remember that in a consonant blend, each consonant sound is pronounced.

A. Look at the the pictures. Say the words out loud. Circle the final blend sounds.

1. band	2. pond	3. plant
4. cent	5. wind	6. hand

B. Read the paragraph out loud. Circle the words with the final blends *nd* and *nt*.

Fred's class went on a trip to the pond. They saw a big plant.

Then they wanted to hunt in the grass to find bugs. They saw

ducks in the pond. One duck did six flips in the sand.

Final Blends: *sp*, *st*, *sk*

> Remember that in a consonant blend, each consonant sound is pronounced.

A. Look at the pictures. Say the words out loud. Circle the final blend sounds.

1.

desk

2.

vest

3.

grasp

4.

mask

5.

nest

6.

wasp

B. Match the rhyming words. Draw a line to show which words rhyme.

1. crisp   task

2. brisk   list

3. ask   west

4. fist   wisp

5. best   disk

High Frequency Words: Set 4

A. You will see these 10 words in many books. Say the words out loud.

go	little	funny	school	have
now	ride	saw	this	want

B. Read the story out loud. Circle the high frequency words.

I ride the school bus every day. I have fun. Yesterday, I saw a little dog. Miss Jen stopped at the STOP sign. The dog walked across the street. I thought this was funny.

I see the school bus now. I want to ride on the bus. I like to go to school.

Name _____ Date _____

Reading Practice: Passage 4

A. Read the story out loud.

What skills do you have? You can look at your skills to pick a job that you like. Stan likes to stack blocks. He can make big stuff. He will like his job. Jen likes to sit in the grass and look at bugs. She can tell us where to find bugs. She wants this fun job. What do you like to do? You can go to school to get a job that you want. You will be glad to have a job that you like.

B. Work with a partner. Answer each question.

1. What is Jen's job?

2. Where can you go to find a job that you like?

 Read the story to a family member or a friend. Discuss the job he or she has now or what job he or she would like to have in the future. What skills are needed for the job?

Initial Digraph: *th*

> A consonant digraph is made up of two consonants that make one sound. The digraph *th* has the first sound in *think*.

A. Look at the pictures. Say the words out loud. Circle the initial digraphs.

1.

three

2.

thumb

B. Circle the words that have the *th* sound. Then read the words out loud.

1. thirteen   tree   thumb

2. top   thirty   thrifty

3. thanks   tanks   tricks

4. theme   think   team

C. Complete each sentence with a word from the box.

then   thick   them

1. What is in that _____ gift?

2. Where are Mom and Dad? I can't see _____.

3. I will pick this one, _____ I will pick that one.

Final Digraph: *th*

> Remember that a consonant digraph is made up of two consonants that make one sound.

A. Look at the pictures. Say the words out loud. Circle the final digraphs.

1.

bath

2.

cloth

3.

moth

4.

sloth

B. Read the words out loud. Circle each word in the word find.

bath	break	cloth	fifth	moth	sloth	wealth

b	a	t	h	z	m	r	l	o	s	c	n
w	r	a	f	c	l	o	t	h	m	k	f
i	w	e	a	l	t	h	t	l	a	e	h
l	h	m	a	s	l	o	t	h	r	t	k
u	n	v	h	k	f	i	f	t	h	b	h

Initial Digraph: *sh*

> Remember that a consonant digraph is made up of two consonants that make one sound.

A. Look at the pictures. Say the words out loud. Circle the initial digraphs.

1.

shell

2.

ship

3.

sheep

4.

shelf

B. Circle the words that have the *sh* sound. Then read the words out loud.

1. shack   shop   thick

2. swim   shed   shell

3. ship   slick   shut

4. thin   shock   shelf

5. sick   sheet   sharp

Final Digraph: *sh*

Remember that a consonant digraph is made up of two consonants that make one sound.

A. Look at the pictures. Say the words out loud. Circle the final digraphs.

1.

brush

2.

fish

3.

cash

4.

dish

B. Circle the words that have *sh* sound. Then read the words out loud.

1. dish   wish   did   **5.** crab   crash   brush

2. cap   trash   tap   **6.** friend   flesh   fresh

3. sip   crush   want   **7.** rash   see   bus

4. Sam   sat   fish   **8.** glass   cash   soup

Name _____ Date _____

Initial Digraphs: *ch, wh*

> Remember that a consonant digraph is made up of two consonants that make one sound.

A. Look at the pictures. Say the words out loud. Circle the initial digraphs.

1.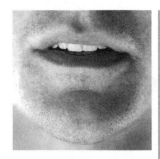

chin

2.

chess

3.

whisk

B. Read the words out loud. Circle each word in the word find.

when	chop	chick	what	check

a	w	h	e	n	c	b	m
c	c	f	b	c	h	u	q
h	d	h	x	e	i	x	w
o	f	r	e	b	c	t	y
p	g	i	j	c	k	p	z
n	w	h	a	t	k	o	n

Name _____ Date _____

Final Digraphs: *ch*, *tch*

> The digraphs *ch* and *tch* have the same sound, as in *which* and *watch*.

A. Look at the pictures. Say the words out loud. Circle the final digraphs.

1.

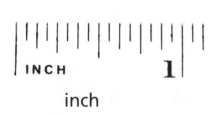

inch

2.

match

3.

lunch

4.

patch

B. Read the words out loud. Circle each word in the word find.

pinch	punch	latch	lunch
patch	catch	witch	munch

c	a	p	p	u	n	c	h	o	m	b	h
u	c	a	t	c	h	c	n	u	r	c	k
m	o	t	q	e	n	u	n	l	n	w	i
e	l	c	w	i	t	c	h	u	g	f	x
n	b	h	p	d	h	z	l	a	t	c	h

Final Digraphs: *ng*, *nk*

> Remember that in a consonant blend, each consonant sound is pronounced.

A. Look at the pictures. Say the words out loud. Circle the final blend sounds.

1.

ring

2.

sink

3.

king

4.

skunk

B. Read the sentences out loud. Underline the words with final blend *ng*. Circle the words with final blend *nk*.

1. Frank likes to sing songs.

2. I am like a king on the top bunk of the bed.

3. One skunk can make the school stink.

4. The dog drank from the sink.

5. Will got a pink ring for his mom.

Chapter 2 Review

A. Pick the best word to finish each sentence. Then write the word.

1. We can (sled, shed) _____ down the hill.

2. Jeff was the (list, last) _____ to come.

3. Dad has to cut the (class, grass) _____.

4. I am (glad, thin) _____ that you are well now.

5. Jan wants to (bring, thing) _____ the hot dog buns.

6. The little (crib, crab) _____ is in the sand.

7. Where will you go on your (chip, trip) _____?

8. The box is (flat, flap) _____ and long.

9. Chad (felt, feld) _____ sick at school.

10. The funny hat was (black, block) _____ and red.

B. Read the story out loud. Fix the spelling of the underlined words.

My class will do a big job at <u>skool</u> _____. We will
_11_

bring plants to the sick. We <u>wissh</u> _____ for them to
_12_

get well. The plants will make <u>thim</u> _____ glad.
_13_

We have ten little red pots of <u>plantts</u> _____.
_14_

"Now we can ride and bring the plants to the sick," said my

mom. We will pack the plants in a van and go on a ride to <u>sheck</u>
_15_

_____ on the sick.

Chapter 2 Review (continued)

C. Fill in the chart below with another word with the same initial blend or digraph.

swap swat **16.** _____	trip trap **17.** _____	cram crush **18.** _____	black blend **19.** _____	flag flip **20.** _____
ship shop **21.** _____	grin grand **22.** _____	prim prom **23.** _____	cling clap **24.** _____	skim skip **25.** _____

D. Read the words out loud. Circle the words that have the same final blend. Underline the blend in each word.

26.   sink   sing   wink

27.   wisp   list   last

28.   melt   belt   weld

29.   send   sent   land

30.   lisp   wasp   mist

Long Vowels

Short *a* and Long *a*

> Sometimes the letter *a* stands for the short vowel sound *a*.
> When a word ends with *a* + consonant + *e*, the letter *a* stands
> for the long vowel /ā/ sound.

A. Look at the pictures. Say the words out loud.

1.

can

2.

cane

◎ **B. Read the words out loud. Draw a line from the short vowel
word to the long vowel word.**

1.	Sal	pale
2.	pal	cape
3.	tap	sale
4.	cap	rate
5.	rat	tape

◎ **C. Circle the word to finish each sentence. Read the sentences
out loud.**

1. Kate was (mad, made) at me.

2. Do you want (tap, tape) for the gift?

3. Where (can, cane) we go?

Name _____   Date _____

Long *a*: *a_e*

> When a word ends with *a* + consonant + *e*, the letter *a* stands for the long vowel /ā/ sound.

A. Look at the pictures. Read the words with long vowel *a* out loud.

1.

cake

2.

tape

3.

gate

B. Read each word out loud. Add *e* to the end of the word and write the new word on the line. Read the new words out loud.

1. fad _____

2. mad _____

3. pan _____

4. Sam _____

C. Complete each sentence with a word from the box.

| cape | tape | snake | skate | same |

1. Jake has a red _____ on his back.

2. He has a pet _____.

3. I can _____ and sing.

4. We can do the _____ things.

5. Let us _____ this here.

Name _____ Date _____

Long *a*: *ay*

> The letters *ay* stand for the long vowel /ā/ sound.

A. Look at the pictures. Read the words with *ay* out loud.

1.
play

2.
hay

3.
clay

B. Read the sentences out loud. Underline the words with *ay*.

1. Your drink is on the tray.

2. Fay said to go this way.

3. I like to play with clay.

4. May I lay this pen on your desk?

5. The gray cat wants to stay here.

C. Complete each sentence with a word from the box.

day	may	stay	pay

1. What _____ will you go to the lake?

2. We will _____ for this snack now.

3. I _____ stop at school to get the bag.

4. This bag will _____ here.

Long *a*: *ai*

The letters *ai* stand for the long vowel /ā/ sound.

A. Look at the pictures. Read the following words with *ai* out loud.

1.

train

2.

braid

3.

snail

B. Add *ai* to the words. Read the words out loud.

1. m____d

2. p____d

3. m____l

4. n____l

5. p____l

6. tr____l

7. m____n

8. p____n

9. dr____n

10. w____st

C. Complete each sentence with a word from the box.

mail	tail	rain

1. Will it _____ on the way to school?

2. Mom got a box in the _____.

3. Jake's dog Bud wags his _____ if he is glad.

Short *o* and Long *o*

> Sometimes the letter *o* stands for the short vowel sound *o*.
> When a word ends with *o* + consonant + *e*, the letter *o*
> stands for the long vowel /ō/ sound.

A. Look at the pictures. Say the words out loud.

1.

tot

2.

tote

◎ **B. Read the words out loud. Write the words in the chart.**

cod	code	cop	cope	nod	node	hop
hope	rod	rode	not	note	mop	mope

Short *o*	Long *o_e*

◎ **C. Complete each sentence with a word from the box. Read the sentences out loud.**

not	jump	hope

1. Did you see the frog _____?

2. I _____ we can play at your home.

3. We did _____ see Pam.

Name _____ Date _____

Long *o*: *o_e*

When a word ends with *o* + consonant + *e*, the letter *o* stands for the long vowel /ō/ sound.

A. Look at the pictures. Read the words with long vowel *o* out loud.

1.

home

2.

globe

3.

hose

B. Read the words out loud. Circle the word with long vowel /ō/ sound.

1. hop   hope

2. note   not

3. tot   tote

4. rode   rod

5. slop   slope

C. Read the letter out loud. Underline all words with long vowel /ō/ sound.

Dear Mr. Rose,

    I want to thank you for the globe you sent me. I will look at it in my home. I like your note, too. I can't wait to tell my friends!

From,
Cole

Name _____ Date _____

Long *o*: *oa*

> The letters *oa* can stand for the long vowel /ō/ sound.

A. Look at the pictures. Read the words with *oa* out loud.

1.

boat

2.

soap

3.

coat

B. Read the words out loud. Draw a line to match the rhyming words.

1. croak   moat
2. road   soak
3. loan   foal
4. coat   toad
5. goal   groan

C. Read the sentences out loud. Underline the words with *oa*.

1. One toad croaks at the pond.

2. I want to soak in the tub with lots of soap.

3. Joan will groan when she drops the pan.

4. I can boast that I made one goal at the game.

5. The bank gave Trent a loan to get a boat.

Name _____ Date _____

Long *o*: *ow*

> The letters *ow* can stand for the long vowel /ō/ sound.

A. Look at the pictures. Read the words with *ow* out loud.

1.

blow

2.

tow

3.

grow

B. Add *ow* to the letters. Read the words out loud.

1. m_____

2. r_____

3. sh_____

4. cr_____

5. fl_____

6. sn_____

C. Change the rhyme with another *ow* word instead of the word *row*. Write it on the line. Be creative! Read your rhyme out loud.

Row, row, row your boat.

_____

Long *o*: *o*, *oe*

The letter *o* can stand for the long vowel /ō/ sound. The letters *oe* can also stand for the long vowel /ō/ sound.

A. Look at the pictures. Read the words with *o* and *oe* out loud.

1.

go

2.

hoe

3.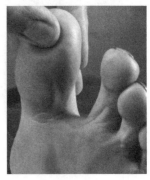

toe

B. Read the words out loud. Circle the two rhyming words.

1. toe   Joe   to

2. go   got   no

3. pro   so   pop

4. do   foe   row

C. Read the sentences out loud. Circle words with *o*. Underline words with *oe*.

1. No, I will not go with you.

2. The tray fell on Joe's toe.

3. It will help if we have a hoe and a rake.

4. It is so hot here.

Name _____ Date _____

High Frequency Words: Set 5

A. You will see these 10 words in many books. Say the words out loud.

two	three	four	blue	yellow
were	was	there	our	please

B. Read the story out loud. Circle the high frequency words.

Jake the snake was at the pond. There he saw two red frogs, three yellow fish, and four blue bugs at play. Jake went up to the two red frogs and said, "Please, can I play with you?"

"Our mom said to come home. We have to go," said the two red frogs. Jake went to the three yellow fish. "Please, can I play with you?"

"Our dad is at home. We have to go there," said the three yellow fish.

The four blue bugs were still there. Jake said, "Please, can I play with you? The two red frogs and three yellow fish had to go home."

"Fine!" they said. Jake was glad.

"Go there," said the four blue bugs. The pond was so much fun for Jake.

Reading Practice: Passage 5

A. Read the story out loud.

> Jane wants to play a game. So she went to find her two pals, Flo and Jim. "Please play a game with me," she said.
>
> Flo and Jim said, "Show us what to do."
>
> So Jane shows them what to do. "The goal is to kick this ball into the yellow net," she said.
>
> Flo and Jim were glad. "That does look like fun. One, two, three! Let us play!" they said.

B. Work with a partner. Answer each question.

1. What does Jane want to do with Flo and Jim?

2. What game do you think they will play?

Home-School Connection Read the story to a family member or a friend. Discuss your favorite sports. Do you both like to play the same games?

Name _____ Date _____

Short *i* and Long *i*

> Sometimes the letter *i* stands for the short vowel /ĭ/ sound. When a word ends with *i* + consonant + *e*, the letter *i* stands for the long vowel /ī/ sound.

A. Look at the pictures. Say the words out loud.

1.

   twin

2.

   twine

B. Read the words with short *i*. Add *e* to the end to make words with long vowel *i*. Write the word on the line. Read the words out loud.

1. hid _____

4. quit _____

2. dim _____

5. fin _____

3. bit _____

6. pin _____

C. Read the sentences out loud. Circle the words with short *i*. Underline the words with long vowel *i*.

1. Tim likes to hide the eggs for the hunt.

2. There are five pins in that cup.

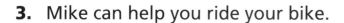

3. Mike can help you ride your bike.

4. I can sit and smell the pine at the park.

Long *i*: *i_e*

> When a word ends with *i* + consonant + *e*, the letter *i* stands for the long vowel /ī/ sound.

A. Look at the pictures. Read the words with long *i* out loud.

1.	2.	3.

bike	smile	dime

B. Read the words out loud. Circle the words in the word find.

hike	shine	smile	time	wipe

```
d   e   t   s   g   h
i   k   i   h   l   m
n   s   m   i   l   e
o   p   e   n   s   t
w   i   p   e   w   d
e   f   h   i   k   e
```

C. Read each sentence out loud. Circle the word that best completes each sentence.

1. Mike has a big (smile, smell).

2. I can hike (fun, five) miles to the top of the hill.

3. The back (tire, top) on his bike broke.

Name _____ Date _____

Long *i*: *igh*

> The letters *igh* stand for the long vowel /ī/ sound.

A. Look at the pictures. Read the words with *igh* out loud.

1.

light

2.

night

3.

bright

B. Add *igh* to complete the words in the sentences. Read the sentences out loud.

1. At n_____t, I like to look way up h_____h.

2. That br_____t l_____t is coming from down there.

3. The blue pants are t_____t on the Kn_____t.

C. Complete each sentence with a word from the box.

| high   right   flight   tight   fight |

1. The rope fits _____ on the rock.

2. I hope our kite will go _____.

3. Tell us the _____ way to go.

4. She does not want to _____ with you.

5. Our _____ lands at nine.

Long *i*: *ie*

The letters *ie* stand for the long vowel /ī/ sound.

A. Look at the pictures. Read the words with *ie* out loud.

1.

pie

2.

tie

B. Read the words out loud. Underline *ie* in each word.

1. die

2. lie

3. flies

4. pie

5. tie

6. cries

C. Read the sentences out loud. Circle words with *ie*.

1. Please lie down in this bed.

2. Do not tell a lie.

3. Kate makes good pies.

4. We gave Dad a red neck tie.

5. Tom tries to play our little game.

Long *i*: *y*

> The letter *y* stands for the long vowel /ī/ sound at the end of some words.

A. Look at the pictures. Read the words with *y* out loud.

1.

cry

2.

sky

B. Complete the sentences with a word from the box.

by	my	dry	shy	why

1. _____ is the sky blue?

2. My swim suit is _____ .

3. The paint is right _____ the desk.

4. Dave is _____ at school.

5. Please come to _____ home.

C. Read the rhyme out loud. Complete the rhyme by adding a word with *y* at the end.

Way up high
In the big, big sky
Joe tried to fly his kite.

He tried and tried,
But it did not go high.
My, little Joe can _____ !

Long *i*: *i*

> The letter *i* can stand for the long vowel /ī/ sound.

A. Look at the pictures. Read the words with *i* out loud.

1.
   blind

2.
   wild

B. Add long vowel *i* to complete the words. Read the words out loud.

1. ch _____ ld

2. f _____ nd

3. k _____ nd

4. m _____ ld

5. gr _____ nd

6. w _____ ld

C. Complete the sentences with a word from the box. Read the sentences out loud.

kind   wind   find   mild   mind

1. What _____ of dog do you have?

2. Please _____ up the jack-in-the-box for Tim.

3. The sun was _____ and bright.

4. Where can we _____ five dimes?

5. I will not _____ if we are late for school.

Name _____ Date _____

Short *u* and Long *u*

Sometimes the letter *u* stands for the short vowel sound /u/. When a word ends with *u* + consonant + *e*, the letter *u* stands for the long vowel /ū/ sound.

A. Look at the pictures. Say the words out loud.

1.
   cub

2.
   cube

B. Complete each sentence with a word from the box.

tub   cut   cute   tube

1. Jess _____ his leg on his bike.

2. Did you see the _____ little cat?

3. Joe has a bath in the _____.

4. A hose is a long _____.

C. Read the words out loud. Write the words in the chart.

plum   rude   cub   tube   cute
tune   fun   mule   smug   flute

Words with Short Vowel *u*	Words with Long Vowel *u*

Long *u*: *u_e*

> When a word ends with *u* + consonant + *e*, the letter *u* stands for the long vowel /ū/ sound.

A. Look at the pictures. Read the words with long vowel *u* out loud.

1.

mule

2.

cube

B. Read the words out loud. Draw a line to match the rhyming words.

1.	rude	plume
2.	rule	dude
3.	fume	flute
4.	June	mule
5.	cute	tune

C. Read the sentences out loud. Circle the best word to complete each sentence.

1. I play the (flute, flume) in the band.

2. May I (cube, use) your bat and mitt?

3. June can play a (dune, tune) on the drum.

4. The mule at the farm was (cut, cute).

5. Matt made a (cube, cub) shape with his clay.

Name _____ Date _____

Long *oo*

> The letters *oo* can stand for the long vowel /ū/ sound.

A. Look at the pictures. Read the words with *oo* out loud.

1.

food

2.

broom

3.

spoon

B. Read the words out loud. Write a rhyming word beside each word.

1. pool _____

3. room _____

2. mood _____

4. troop _____

C. Complete the sentences with a word from the box.

| groom | noon | moon | roof | pool |

1. The bride and _____ ate the cake.

2. The _____ was bright last night.

3. Shane can swim in the _____.

4. The crow's nest is on the _____.

5. At _____ we will have lunch.

High Frequency Words: Set 6

A. You will see these 10 words in many books. Say the words out loud.

live	who	these	friend	give
put	new	away	could	her

B. Read the story out loud. Circle the high frequency words in the story.

Mom and I went to the Shoe Shop close to where we live to find new rain boots. We saw our friend Jess there.

"Mom, could I try these on? Or could I try those on?" I said. I went to give her the new boots, but she put them away.

"Who could walk in the rain with these? They are too low," she said.

I walk away and look for high boots. "Jess saw these boots, Mom. Could I try them on?"

I give Mom the new boots that I like.

"Yes, these are fine." She put them down so I could try them on. They fit just right.

"Thank you, Jess. What a friend!" I said.

Reading Practice: Passage 6

A. Read the story out loud.

My name is Joan. I like to play the flute. I take a flute class at a school close to my home. I want to play songs and do shows with my friend's band.

At flute class, I learn the right way to play the notes fast. I have to play in tune with the rest of the band. I learn where to put my hand so I can play the notes fast. I play at home, too. Soon I will play well. Then you could come to see our show!

B. Work with a partner. Answer each question.

1. What kind of class does Joan take?

2. What does she want to do?

Home-School Connection Read the story to a family member or a friend. Does he or she play a musical instrument? Do you? Discuss why you like playing your musical instrument.

Name _____   Date _____

Long *e*: *ee*

> The letters *ee* can stand for the long vowel /e/ sound.

A. Look at the pictures. Read the words with *ee* out loud.

1.

bee

2.

tree

B. Add *ee* to complete the words. Read the words out loud.

1. f_____l

2. ch_____k

3. sl_____p

4. s_____

5. t_____th

6. w_____d

C. Read each riddle out loud. Answer each riddle with a word that has *ee*.

1. I am big.
   I am green.
   I give shade when you are hot.
   What am I?

   _____

2. I am on a bed.
   You sleep on me.
   I am not a quilt.
   What am I?

   _____

Long *e*: *ea*

> The letters *ea* can stand for the long vowel /ē/ sound.

A. Look at the pictures. Read the words with *ea* out loud.

1.

beak

2.

read

B. Read the words out loud. Circle the words in the word find.

mean	real	pea	sneak	peach

p	e	a	c	h	g	e
i	k	r	h	l	m	m
n	s	n	e	a	k	e
o	p	e	n	a	t	a
p	e	a	x	w	l	n

C. Read each riddle out loud. Answer each riddle with an *ea* word.

1. I am a place.
   I have sand.
   I have waves.
   What am I?

   _____

2. I have food.
   I have drinks.
   Lots will come when I am here.
   What am I?

   _____

Short *e* and Long *e*

> Sometimes the letter *e* stands for the short vowel e sound.
> The letters *ee* and *ea* stand for the long vowel /ē/ sound.

A. Look at the pictures. Say the words out loud.

1.

ten

2.

teen

B. Read the sentences out loud. Circle the word that best completes each sentence.

1. Can I have (meat, met) with my eggs?

2. We need (ten, tweed) men to take that truck away.

3. There was one (pea, pen) left on his plate.

C. Read the words out loud. Write them in the chart.

bee	bet	flea	flee	sweet	set	wet	treat
ten	when	read	bead	beach	meal	jet	men

Short *e*	Long *e*

Long e: *ie*

Sometimes the letters *ie* stand for the long vowel /ē/ sound.

A. Look at the pictures. Read the following words with *ie* out loud.

1.  **2.**  **3.**

field   yield   briefcase

B. Add *ie* to complete the words. Read the words out loud.

1. br_____f   **4.** y_____ld

2. gr_____f   **5.** ch_____f

3. f_____ld   **6.** n_____ce

C. Read the sentences out loud. Underline the words with *ie*.

1. We want to put new lines on the field.

2. There is a yield sign by the school.

3. Ms. Lee needs to make a brief speech.

4. My friend wants to be the chief.

5. James felt grief when his dog ran away.

High Frequency Words: Set 7

A. You will see these 10 words in many books. Say the words out loud.

after	going	how	been	done
very	or	under	always	because

B. Read the story out loud. Circle the high frequency words in the story.

Do you always have dreams when you sleep? Do you wake up because of dreams? One time, I woke up after a dream and I felt sad. I am going to ask my friend to tell me why we dream.

She said that when we sleep, we rest and can go in to a very deep sleep. This is the state of REM sleep. This is the time when we dream. When you are in REM sleep, it is like you are under a spell. If you wake up when you dream, it might not be done and you can tell your mom or dad how it was going.

You might think you do not dream when you sleep, but we always do. If you do have a dream, it may seem like it has been very real. It may seem like you are going to cry or run or drive, but the whole thing was just a dream.

The next time you have a dream, here is what you can do: After you wake up, always jot the dream down. Then you can read it the next day.

Name _____ Date _____

Reading Practice: Passage 7

A. Read the story out loud.

My class is going to clean our play field at school. There is always trash on our field, and we want to clean it up.

There is a lot to do. We can pick up cans and junk and put them in bags. Then we can sweep the whole site. After we pick up this stuff, we are going to rake the grass. It needs help to grow. It is yellow now and we want it to be green.

When we are done with our field, we will clean up the beach. The beach has a lot of trash in the sand. We will pick up the stuff and put it in a bag. After we clean the beach, we are going to swim.

This is a big job. We want to do it because we like where we live. We are going to have a lot of fun, too!

B. Work with a partner. Answer each question.

1. What is the class going to clean up?

2. Why does the class want to clean up these things?

Home-School Connection Read the story to a family member or a friend. Discuss ways you can help keep your neighborhood or play fields clean and neat.

CVCe Syllables and Phonograms

Many words have the consonant-vowel-consonant-silent *e* or CVCe syllable pattern. CVCe words most often are phonograms. Phonograms are one-syllable words that can be grouped by word families.

A. Read the CVCe word families out loud.

-ate	-ine	-ole	-une
date	dine	mole	dune
late	mine	pole	June
rate	nine	role	tune

B. Read the sentences out loud. Circle the CVCe words.

1. June went to bed late last night.

2. We like to smell the pine trees at Gram's home.

3. There are nine friends going at the same time.

4. We gave cake to the kids by the lake.

5. Jake gave a speech at the school's new gate.

C. Fill in the chart with another word in each word family.

-ame	-ope	-ive	-use
came	mope	five	muse
_____	_____	_____	_____
-ade	**-one**	**-ide**	**-ute**
shade	bone	side	cute
_____	_____	_____	_____

CVVC Syllables (Vowel Teams)

> Some words have the consonant-vowel-vowel-consonant or CVVC syllable pattern. CVVC syllables have vowel teams, or two vowels put together. Often the vowel teams make a long vowel sound.

A. Read the words with CVVC syllables out loud.

-ai (long a)	-ea (long e)	-ee (long e)	-oa (long o)
paid	read	deep	road
laid	clean	peep	toad
rain	steam	weep	boat

B. Read the rhyme out loud. Circle the words that have a CVVC syllable pattern.

There a was a sailboat, little and clean,

That could ride on the blue sea.

One day a steamboat came by.

He said, "I wish that could be me."

The steamboat saw him and he said,

"Come and sail with me,"

The little sailboat got a clean rope

And he put it in the sea.

The steamboat held the rope for him,

And they rode so fast and free.

The sailboat was so very glad.

"Thanks!" said the little boat "Whee!"

Chapter 3 Review

A. Circle the word that best completes each sentence. Read the sentences out loud.

1. I (mad, made) my mom a cake.

2. I (hope, hop) she likes it.

3. "(Try, Tray) it!" I said. "I made it by myself."

4. "This is the best," said Mom, as she had it on a (spin, spoon).

5. "But you gave me (too, two) much," she said.

6. Mom (at, ate) a bit of the cake and left the rest.

7. I ate the rest off of her (plate, plot) with my hands.

8. "It was (sweet, sent) of you to make that cake for me," she said with a smile.

9. Then she made me (clean, clip) up the mess in the sink.

10. Moms can be so (mean, men)!

B. Read the story out loud. Correct the underlined words.

My firend _____ likes to paint mugs. When
    11

the mugs are dry, she allways _____ gives them
               12

away. She will use blew _____ and pink to paint
          13

a mug for hur _____ mom. She wants to keep
       14

this one beecause _____ she likes pink the best.
        15

Chapter 3 Review (continued)

C. Circle the words in the word find.

16. crow	r	s	h	o	w	c	t
17. least	p	m	i	t	e	r	h
18. speech	r	i	l	h	u	o	i
19. thief	r	e	d	e	a	w	e
20. show	n	g	p	m	a	d	f
21. soon	g	o	r	e	a	s	e
22. theme	s	p	e	e	c	h	t
	s	o	o	n	d	a	d

D. Read the words out loud. Circle the words that have the same long vowel sound. Underline the letters that spell the long vowel in each word.

23.	meet	team	fright
24.	sit	slide	sight
25.	make	maid	soap
26.	braid	bleed	stay
27.	lie	hope	soap
28.	tune	mail	gloom
29.	yield	ride	steam
30.	chime	grow	toe

Contractions and Inflections

Name _____ Date _____

Syllables

> A syllable is a word or part of a word that has a vowel sound. You can count syllables by looking at the number of vowel sounds in a word, or by counting the number of times your mouth opens when you say a word.

A. Look at the pictures. Say the words out loud. Count the number of syllables.

1.

briefcase

2.

July

3.

dime

B. Read the words out loud. Count the syllables in each word. Circle the vowel sounds.

1. napkin

2. kitten

3. class

4. yellow

C. Read the sentences out loud. Circle the words that have two syllables.

1. Please give me my new backpack.

2. They have to cross the railroad tracks to get to the seashore.

3. We are going home after our hike up the hill.

4. Kids can play games on the blacktop at school.

5. Brad is going to take me to the beach.

Inflections: *-ed*, *-ing*

> The inflection *-ed* is added to a word to change it into the simple past. The inflection *-ing* is added to a word to change it into a present participle. Use a form of the verb *be* + a present participle to form the present progressive tense.

A. Read the words out loud.

Base Word	Simple Past	Present Participle
pick	picked	picking
1 syllable	1 syllable	2 syllables

B. Draw a line to match each base word to the simple past form of the word.

Base Word	Simple Past
1. fix	missed
2. pack	fixed
3. tick	packed
4. lock	ticked
5. miss	locked

C. Finish each sentence with the present participle (*-ing* form) of the word.

1. Pam is (pick) _____ up the clothes.

2. Drake is (miss) _____ his blue bike.

3. Tom's cat is (lick) _____ his hand.

4. Dad is (mix) _____ the eggs and milk.

5. Jean is (pack) _____ a bag to go away.

Inflections: *-ed, -ing*

Some short vowel words end with a single consonant. If *-ed* or *-ing* is added, double the consonant at the end and then add the inflection.

A. Read the examples out loud.

Past Tense	Present Participle
jog + ed = jogged	jog + ing= jogging
tip + ed = tipped	tip + ing = tipping
bat + ed = batted	bat + ing = batting

B. Read the words out loud. Fill in the blank with either the simple past or the present participle (*-ing form*) of the word.

1. pat   patted   _____

2. beg   _____   begging

3. tug   _____   tugging

4. trim   trimmed   _____

5. nod   nodded   _____

C. Read the sentences out loud. Correct the underlined words.

1. Pat was <u>swating</u> the bugs at night. _____

2. Mom <u>huged</u> me. _____

3. Are you <u>diging</u> in the mud with your hand? _____

4. Tim <u>joged</u> down the lane. _____

5. Joe was <u>siting</u> on the side of the crate. _____

Inflections: *-ed, -ing*

Many long vowel words end with e. If an inflection is added, the e is dropped and then *-ed* or *-ing* is added.

A. Read the examples out loud.

Past Tense	Present Participle
save + ed = saved	save + ing = saving
note + ed = noted	note + ing = noting

B. Read the words in the chart out loud. Fill in the blank with the base word, simple past, or present participle (*-ing*) form of the word.

Base Word	Present Participle	Simple Past
joke	joking	_____
_____	baking	baked
shape	_____	shaped
vote	_____	voted
slope	sloping	_____

C. Read each sentence out loud. Correct the underlined words.

1. I was <u>hopeing</u> that you come. _____

2. Jake <u>saveed</u> me this cake. _____

3. I am <u>takking</u> him home. _____

4. My mom <u>votted</u> today. _____

High Frequency Words: Set 8

A. You will see these 10 words in many books. Say the words out loud.

their	about	full	would	laugh
many	only	again	buy	know

B. Read the story out loud. Underline the high frequency words in the story.

Jake and his friends went to the beach. They had their pails with them. They put sand in their pails until they were full. Then they would dump the wet sand in a row. They did this again and again.

There were so many piles of sand. Jake's friend Jack did not know what they were making. He asked Jake again and again, and he would just laugh. Jake went to buy a hot dog, and Jack asked his friends about the sand piles. They would only laugh, too.

When Jake came back, Jack asked about the piles one more time. Jake said, "We are only making a heap, Jack! Do you want to help?"

Name _____ Date _____

Reading Practice: Passage 8

A. Read the story out loud.

A fish can be a fossil. How could a fish be a fossil? It takes a long time. When a fish dies, it sinks down to the bottom of the sea. It is under the sand for a very long time. The sand becomes rock. The soft spots of the fish waste away. Only the bones are left. The fish's bones become hard like rock. The bones are the only things we see in that rock.

If you find a fossil, see what is left of the fish that died. Share the fossil with your classmates and family.

B. Work with a partner. Answer each question.

1. Does a fish become a fossil in a little or long time?

2. What is left from the fish that you can see in a fossil?

Home-School Connection Read the story to a family member or a friend. Have either of you ever found a fossil? What would you do if you found a fossil?

Contractions with *not*

A contraction is a single word made by combining two words. The contraction *can't* is made by combining *can* and *not*. The two words are joined with an apostrophe (').

A. Read these contractions made with the word *not* out loud.

will not = won't	did not = didn't	do not = don't
is not = isn't	have not = haven't	does not = doesn't
cannot = can't	must not = mustn't	

B. Complete each sentence with a contraction.

1. I (did not) _____ go to school today.

2. I (will not) _____ go to school on the next day.

3. I (cannot) _____ miss too many days.

4. I (have not) _____ had chicken pox.

5. It (is not) _____ so bad getting sick.

6. Many kids (must not) _____ be next to me right now.

C. Read the sentences out loud. Underline the contractions. Then rewrite each sentence using two words instead of the contraction.

1. "Don't be mean," he said. "Can't you lend me ten dollars?"

_____

2. "I would if I could, but I can't so I won't," she said.

_____

Name _____ Date _____

Contractions with *will*

The contraction *I'll* is made by combining *I* and *will*. The two words are joined with an apostrophe ('). Contractions with *will* are used to talk about the future.

A. Read these contractions made with the word *will* out loud.

I will = I'll   you will = you'll   she will = she'll
he will = he'll   it will = it'll   they will = they'll
we will = we'll

B. Complete each sentence with a contraction from the box.

1. Give the box to me. _____ take it to Miss Marks.

2. Miss Marks will thank me. _____ be glad to get the box from me.

3. We will open it after lunch. Then _____ show our friends what is inside.

4. We will tell our parents and _____ be happy to know about our day.

C. Read the story out loud. If the underlined contraction is correct, write C. If it is wrong, write the correct contraction.

Mrs. Kind will be visiting soon. <u>Shel'l</u> _____ bring

1

her fat cat, Bandit. <u>I'll</u> _____ let the cat sleep on my

2

feet to keep them snug. <u>Hel'l</u> _____ sleep so well that

3

night. The next day, <u>Ill</u> _____ play with the cat. <u>We'll</u>

4   5

_____ have a fun time!

Contractions with *would*

> The contraction *she'd* is made by combining *she* and *would*.
> The two words are joined with an apostrophe (').

A. Read these contractions made with the word *would* out loud.

I would = I'd	you would = you'd	she would = she'd
he would = he'd	it would = it'd	we would = we'd
they would = they'd		

B. Complete each sentence with a contraction.

1. (I would) _____ like to visit the zoo one day.

2. Mom could take us. (She would) _____ like to drive there.

3. (We would) _____ have a fun time at the zoo.

4. (It would) _____ be fun to see the seals.

C. Read the story out loud. If the underlined contraction is correct, write C. If it is wrong, write the correct contraction.

<u>I'd</u> _____ like to live under the sea. <u>Itw'd</u>
  1   2

_____ be neat to be with those fish. <u>They'wd</u>
                                                          3

_____ swim next to me, and <u>I'dd</u> _____
                                                         4

swim as fast as them. <u>Youw'd</u> _____ like it, too. <u>W'ed</u>
                              5   6

_____ laugh and play the day away in our blue world.

Contractions with *have*

> The contraction *I've* is made by combining *I* and *have*.
> The two words are joined with an apostrophe (').

A. Read these contractions made with the word *have* out loud.

I have = I've	you have = you've
we have = we've	they have = they've

B. Replace each underlined phrase with a contraction from the box.

1. Look at that blue jay! <u>You have</u> _____ got to see it!

2. I think its wing is bent. Let's get a box. <u>You and I have</u> _____ got to save it.

3. <u>The men at the desk have</u> _____ got to help us.

4. <u>You and I have</u> _____ saved a bird.

C. Read the rhyme out loud. If the underlined contraction is correct, write C. If it is wrong, write the correct contraction.

<u>I've</u> _____ just cracked my book and <u>you'have</u> _____
  1   2

come here with your drum. <u>Wev'e</u> _____ got to think. Stop
                             3

and look. I can read and you can hum.

Contractions with *are*

> The word *are* can be used in contractions to talk about more than one person. The contraction *we're* is made by combining *we* and *are*.

A. Read these contraction made with the word *are* out loud.

you are = you're	we are = we're	they are = they're

B. Circle the best contraction to complete each sentence.

1. James, (you're / we're) my best friend.

2. (We're / They're) going to the next game. Dad can take us.

3. The chess club will sell milk shakes. (They're / We're) going to sell hot dogs, too.

4. (You're / We're) in the mood for a milk shake, are you not?

5. I don't like milk shakes. (They're / We're) too sweet for me.

C. Look at the contractions you circled in Exercise B. Write the two words that each contraction stands for.

1. _____   _____

2. _____   _____

3. _____   _____

4. _____   _____

5. _____   _____

Contractions with *is*

The word *is* can be used in contractions. Use it with nouns and pronouns. Join the two words with an apostrophe (').

A. Read these contractions made with the word *is* out loud.

he is = he's	she is = she's	it is = it's
that is = that's	what is = what's	Mom is = Mom's

B. Finish each sentence with a contraction from the box.

1. Mr. Childs is my boss. _____ always making me laugh.

2. _____ my desk. What a mess!

3. _____ always getting piled up with stuff.

4. I can't wait to show my mom. _____ going to smile.

5. Mom, _____ for lunch?

C. Read the story out loud. Circle the correct contraction.

Tom: "Look what I have, Mom!"

Mom: "(What's / That's) this?"
          1

Tom: "(He's / It's) my test. Look at it."
          2

Mom: "(She's / That's) a fine grade! Way to go!"
          3

Contractions with *'s* and Possessive *'s*

> The apostrophe can be used to show possession. Pronouns don't use possessive *'s*.

A. Read the sentences.

1. **Jim's** dog ran away. (**The dog that belongs to Jim** ran away.)

2. The coat is **hers**. (*not* The coat is her's.)

3. The pen is **yours**. (*not* The pen is your's.)

4. The dog licked **its** nose. (*not* The dog licked it's nose.)

B. Never form a plural with an apostrophe. Read the sentences.

1. The **hens** came home. (*not* The hen's came home.)

2. The **cats** are down there. (*not* The cat's are down there.)

C. Read the story out loud. Correct the spelling errors.

Jacks _____ dog, Ben, likes to go visiting the kids
    1

on the block. As soon as they get home, Ben runs away. Jack's dad

doesn't like when he does this. The kid's _____ on
                                              2

the block like Ben's visit's _____. He licks their hand's
                                3   4

_____. The kids think hes' _____ such a
                                              5

cute dog!

Name _____ Date _____

Long e: *ey, y*

The letters *ey* and *y* can stand for the long vowel /ē/ sound.
Words with *y* are usually two-syllable words.

A. Look at the pictures. Read the words with *ey* and *y* out loud.

1.

keys

2.

alley

3.

family

B. Read the words out loud. Underline *ey* or *y* in each word.

1. body

2. copy

3. penny

4. many

5. funny

6. puppy

7. happy

8. key

C. Complete each sentence with a word from the box. Read the sentences out loud.

    happy   kitty   key   very

1. The _____ rubbed my leg.

2. I need a _____ to lock the gate.

3. Abby is _____ that she is in the play.

4. A snake can be _____ soft.

Inflections: *-ed*, *-es*, *-ing*

> To add an inflection to a base word that ends with *y*, change the *y* to *i* and add *-ed* or *-es*. Keep the *y* when adding *-ing* to the word.

A. Read the examples out loud.

Simple Past	Present Participle
study + ed= studied	study + ing = studying
	study + es = studies

B. Complete the chart.

Base Word	*-ed*	*-es*	*-ing*
fly	flied	flies	_____
try	_____	tries	trying
cry	cried	_____	crying
_____	dried	dries	drying
fry	fried	fries	_____

C. Read the story out loud. Correct the underlined words.

I am (1) <u>studing</u> to fly a plane. I would like to try (2) <u>flyying</u> when I grow up. As a jet or a plane (3) <u>flyes</u> by, I look up in the blue (4) <u>skyes</u> and dream. There is no (5) <u>denyying</u> it, that is what I want to be.

1. _____   **4.** _____

2. _____   **5.** _____

3. _____

Inflections: *-er*, *-est*

> To compare two things, add *-er* to the end of an adjective. Use the word *than* to compare the two things. If the word ends in a *y*, change the *y* to *i* before adding *-er*.

A. Read the sentences out loud.

1. The red paint is **brighter** than the blue paint.

2. That joke was **funnier** than the last one.

> To compare three or more things, add *-est* to the end of an adjective. If it ends in a *y*, change the *y* to *i* before adding *-est*.

B. Read the sentences out loud.

1. I have three ducks. The yellow one is the **longest**.

2. It is the **happiest** of the three ducks, too.

> If the word ends in a single consonant, double the final consonant to keep the vowel short.

C. Read the sentences out loud.

1. That film was **sadder** than the last one.

2. It is the **saddest** film I have seen yet!

D. Add *-er* or *-est* to the word in parentheses.

1. This time, we stayed in the (fancy) _____ room.

2. It was (big) _____ than the other ones.

3. I slept on the (soft) _____ bed in the room.

High Frequency Words: Set 9

A. You will see these 10 words in many books. Say the words out loud.

some	before	work	pretty	any
walk	also	over	never	says

B. Read the story out loud. Underline the high frequency words in the story.

I like to see my friend before I walk to school. She works over at the pet shop. Any time I ask her to help, she never says no.

Some days, I get to help her clean the snake tanks. That's so much fun. I also play with the pretty white rabbit when I am there. The pet shop doesn't have any cats.

My friend says that I'm a fine helper. It doesn't seem like work to me when I clean the tanks or play with the pets. Someday, I'd also like to get paid to stay with the pets. After I help her, I have to walk to school. Some days, I go back over to the pet shop after school, too.

Reading Practice: Passage 9

A. Read the story out loud.

Our team is the Jets. We play on the west field after school. The moms and dads come to cheer us on. My mom, my biggest fan, always comes to the games. Her cheers help me to run faster.

We have a coach named Ben. He makes us run and stretch. He makes us do squats until our legs shake. We moan a lot of the time, but thanks to this training, we are fast and strong. The Jets are the team to beat.

I like playing with my team. We are the fastest and strongest of the teams we play. We always try to do our best. I like to feel the sun on my skin and grime on my hands. I also like the smell of a mitt and the feel of a bat. This is my game.

B. Work with a partner. Answer each question.

1. What game does the team play?

2. What is the name of the team?

Home-School Connection Read the story to a family member or a friend. Does he or she play a team sport? Discuss sports you both like to play.

Name _____ Date _____

Chapter 4 Review

A. Complete each sentence with a word from the box.

candy	laugh	Only	waiting	would
know	over	after	work	alley

1. When do you want to come _____ to my place?

2. I can be there _____ I eat.

3. My mom gets home from _____ at six.

4. Do you think she _____ give me a ride home?

5. Yes, I _____ that will be fine.

6. I will meet you by the _____ .

7. Can you please be there _____ for me?

8. _____ if you're on time.

9. Okay! I'll bring some _____ for us to eat.

10. We'll eat and _____ while we study.

B. Read the story out loud. Correct the underlined words.

It's been raining all day. Today is the <u>rainier</u> _____ day of
                                          11

the week. The grass is <u>greenest</u> _____ than last week. Things
                          12

look <u>cleanest</u> _____ and <u>brightest</u> _____ . But not our
        13   14

dog. He played in the <u>deeper</u> _____ mud hole he could find.
                          15

He's the <u>muddyest</u> _____ dog on the block. He's <u>happyest</u>
             16   17

_____ when he's muddy.

Name _____ Date _____

Chapter 4 Review (continued)

C. Complete each sentence with a contraction. Read the sentences out loud.

18. I (cannot) _____ see very well.

19. I hope I (do not) _____ need glasses.

20. I (would not) _____ mind getting cool glasses.

21. Cool glasses (are not) _____ so bad.

22. Steve got glasses last week. He (does not) _____ like them.

23. He says they (do not) _____ feel right.

24. (He is) _____ not going to let his mom choose his glasses again.

25. (I will) _____ go with him when he goes to pick new ones.

26. (I would) _____ like to get cool black frames.

27. (We would) _____ use our glasses in school.

D. Add -ed or -ing to the underlined words. Write them on the lines.

28. I <u>pick</u> these pretty roses for you. _____

29. She has been <u>wait</u> here for a long time. _____

30. I <u>like</u> meeting your mom. _____

31. I am <u>paint</u> the frame black. _____

32. I didn't know you <u>want</u> to come with us. _____

More Vowel Patterns

Blends with Three Letters: *str*, *spl*, *scr*

When a word begins with a consonant blend, two or three consonants are blended together. You hear each consonant sound in the blend.

A. Read these words with three-letter blends out loud.

strap   splash   scrub

B. Complete each sentence with a word from the box. Read the sentences out loud.

scrap	scrape	split	string	strong

1. Dad can _____ that log in two with an ax.

2. My dad is very _____, so he can lift the log.

3. The one that is left over is just a _____.

4. Dad ties the sticks with thick _____.

5. Sometimes Dad gets a _____ on his hand from the sticks.

C. Read the clues. Add *scr*, *spl*, or *str* to complete the words. Read the words out loud.

1. to cut something in two   _____ it

2. not weak   _____ong

3. to clean well   _____ub

4. where trucks drive   _____eet

5. don't play in the tub or you will   _____ash

Digraph Blends: *shr*, *thr*

When a word begins with *shr* or *thr*, pronounce the *sh* and *th* digraphs separately.

A. Read these words with digraph blends out loud.

shrug   shrimp   three   throw

B. Complete each sentence with a word from the box. Read the sentences out loud.

shred	shrub	throat	throw

1. A little bush is a _____.

2. I don't want anyone to see these checks, so I'll _____ them.

3. Don't _____ that away, please.

4. I am sick and my _____ is red.

C. Read the clues. Write the word from the box that each clue tells about.

thrill	shrimp	shrink	three	throne

1. before four _____

2. a cool ride _____

3. seafood _____

4. a king sits on this _____

5. to make little _____

Name _____   Date _____

R-controlled /är/: *ar*

When an *a* is followed by a single *r*, the vowel sound is neither long or short. The *a* makes a special sound. The *a* is called an *r*-controlled vowel.

A. Look at the pictures. Say the words out loud.

1.

card

2.

star

B. Add *ar* to finish the words. Read the words out loud.

1. f_____   4. st_____t

2. _____m   5. h_____d

3. c_____t   6. sm_____rt

C. Finish each sentence with a word from the box. Read the sentences out loud.

market	barn	tart	March

1. The spring _____ started today.

2. It is being held in the big red _____.

3. February is the month before _____.

4. You can get _____ plums at the spring market.

Name _____ Date _____

R-controlled /ôr/: *or, ore, our*

> When a vowel (or vowels) is followed by a single *r*,
> the vowel has a special sound. The vowel is called an
> *r*-controlled vowel.

A. Look at the pictures. Say the words out loud.

1.

corn

2.

store

3.

four

B. Complete each sentence with a word from the box. Read the sentences out loud.

pour	more	storm	your

1. I am having so much fun at _____ party.

2. Would you please _____ me a glass of milk?

3. I want to have one _____ glass.

4. The sky got dark. I think that there might be a _____.

C. Read this ad out loud. Underline the words with /ôr/ spelled *or, our,* or *ore*.

Do you like going to the store to get more food?
It's such a chore. Do you like to eat? Of course you do!
In that case, let Lenore do it for you.
She can bring a four-course meal to your home.
All you need is a fork!

Name _____   Date _____

R-controlled /ür/: *er, ir, ur*

> When a vowel is followed by a single *r*, the vowel has a
> special sound. The vowel is called an *r*-controlled vowel.
> The letters *er, ir,* and *ur* make the /ür/ sound.

A. Look at the pictures. Say the words out loud.

1.

fern

2.

bird

3.

surf

**B. Complete each sentence with a word from the box. Read the
sentences out loud.**

perch	hurt	turn	skirt

1. On Sunday, we saw a bird that had a _____ wing.

2. My friend scooped it up in her _____.

3. She said that the bird looked like it fell from its _____.

4. Now we are waiting for our _____ to see the vet.

**C. Read this rhyme out loud. Underline the words that have /ür/
spelled *er, ur,* or *ir.***

She twirls and turns as if on a spring,
The quick, perky girl on the flying swing.
She leaps from her perch and jumps up to fly,
Pretty and free as a bird in the sky.

Name _____ Date _____

R-controlled /ür/: (*earn, work*)

When a vowel (or vowels) is followed by a single *r*, the vowel has a special sound. The vowel is called an *r*-controlled vowel. The letters *ear* and *ar* can sometimes make the /ür/ sound.

A. Look at the pictures. Say the words out loud.

1.

Earth

2.

worm

B. Read the /ür/ words in the box out loud. Circle them in the word find.

| search | worm | earth | work | learn | world | pearl |

m o p e r c a

w r e c w o l

o o a d o l e

r i r c r w a

l t l k m g r

d b m l q r n

o w e a r t h

s e a r c h r

High Frequency Words: Set 10

A. You will see these 10 words in many books. Say the words out loud.

eye	warm	push	carry	together
small	people	favorite	pull	out

B. Read the story out loud. Underline the high frequency words.

I would like to take a trip to my favorite spot in the world, Pearl Beach. In the winter, it is so cold here that I have to carry a scarf when I go out. In Pearl Beach, it is always sunny and warm. Sometimes the sun can be too much for me, but I can pull my hat down to shade my eyes.

I like Pearl Beach because I can get together with my friends and have a small party on the beach. We will have drinks and snacks out on the sand. I will ask people to push me into the warm water so I can swim. We will carry our trash to the bin when we are done. Pearl Beach is my favorite spot on Earth!

Reading Practice: Passage 10

A. Read the story out loud.

Hal jumps out of the plane and floats down. His goal is to reach the flames that burn the dried-out trees and shrubs. The closer he is to the flames, the better. Is Hal nuts? No, he's a smokejumper. He's a well-trained fighter of flames and smoke. He throws dirt on the flames and wets the trees and shrubs so they won't burn.

He works together with a small team of smokejumpers. This team goes to fight the flames that most people can't get to. They reach the wild flames by jumping out of a plane. When word comes in that trees are burning, Hal and his team run to the plane and put on their packs. The plane flies over the trees. The smokejumper waits for the right time. There it is. It's time for Hal and his team to jump out and fight flames and smoke.

B. Work with a partner. Answer each question.

1. What does Hal jump out of?

2. What does Hal do when he gets to the flames?

Home-School Connection Read the story to a family member or a friend. Discuss Hal's dangerous job. Do you think he is brave?

Name _____ Date _____

R-controlled /âr/: *are, air*

> The consonant *r* can change the sound of a long vowel *a*. The /âr/ sound is most commonly spelled *are* and *air*.

A. Look at the pictures. Say the words out loud.

1.

chair

2.

square

3.

stair

B. Complete each sentence with a word from the box. Read the sentences out loud.

hair   scare   fair   pair

1. Would you like to go to the _____ with me?

2. I have a _____ of tickets.

3. I won't go on the fast rides. They _____ me.

4. Besides, I don't want to mess up my _____.

C. Read the clues. Answer with two rhyming words that contain *air* or *are*. The first one is done for you.

1. A seat with nothing in it.   _____ _____

2. Seat with four sides that are that same.   _____ _____

3. two cubes   _____ of _____

CVrC, CVrCe Syllables

When *r* comes after a vowel, it changes the sound of that vowel. Sometimes a silent *e* follows the *r*, but it does not change the sound. The sound remains *r*-controlled.

A. Read the words with CVrCe out loud.

nurse   charge   serve

B. Complete each sentence with a word from the box.

large   purse   thirst   starve

1.   Here is something to quench your _____.

2.   It's a _____ glass of water.

3.   Are you hungry? I don't want you to _____.

4.   You can take this snack and carry it in your _____.

C. Read the words out loud. Circle them in the word find.

garden   shore   murky   nurse   charge   verse   nerve

c	i	n	v	n	w	g	m
h	o	i	e	u	y	a	u
a	r	n	r	r	t	r	r
r	a	e	s	s	v	d	k
g	d	v	e	e	p	e	y
e	u	r	r	s	r	n	m
k	n	c	s	h	o	r	e

Diphthong /*oi*/: *oy, oi*

> The vowel sound /oi/ can be spelled with the vowel team *oi* or *oy*. A vowel team always stays together in the same syllable.

A. Look at the pictures. Say the words out loud.

1.

coins

2.

oil

3.

boy

B. Read the clues. Complete the puzzle with words from the box.

join	toys	broil	boy	employ	enjoy

Across
1. to heat under a flame
2. to give a job to
4. playthings

Down
1. not a girl
2. to like
3. come together

Name _____   Date _____

Vowel Team /ou/: *ou, ow*

> The vowel sound /ou/ can be spelled with the vowel team *ou* or *ow*. A vowel team always stays together in the same syllable.

A. Look at the pictures. Say the words out loud.

1.
cloud

2.
cow

3.
crown

B. Read the words out loud. Circle the letters that make the /ou/ sound.

1. round

2. now

3. clown

4. mouth

5. loud

6. howl

C. Complete each sentence with a word from the box. Read the sentences out loud.

outside	frown	found	brow

1. It was such a nice day that I went _____.

2. In the yard, I _____ a beehive.

3. I got stung on my eye _____.

4. That bee sting made me _____.

Vowel Team /aw/: *aw, au*

> The vowel sound /aw/ can be spelled with the vowel team *aw* or *au*. A vowel team always stays together in the same syllable.

A. Look at the pictures. Say the words out loud.

1.

auto

2.

laundry

3.

saw

B. Read these words out loud. Circle the letters that make the /aw/ sound.

1. launch

3. draw

2. fawn

4. cause

C. Complete each sentence with a word from the box. Read the sentences out loud.

lawn	straw	awful	August	haul

1. In _____, it is very hot outside.

2. Our _____ tends to dry up a bit.

3. Sometimes it looks like _____.

4. Dad says not to _____ out the hose.

5. Our lawn looks _____ in late summer.

Vowel Team /oo/: *ew, ui, oe, oo*

> The vowel sound /oo/ can be spelled with the vowel team *ew, ui, oe,* or *oo*. A vowel team always stays together in the same syllable.

A. Look at the pictures. Say the words out loud.

1.
news

2.
suit

3.
canoe

B. Read words out loud. Circle the letters that make the /oo/ sound.

1. canoe

2. hoot

3. fruit

4. knew

5. chew

6. cruise

7. moon

8. suit

C. Complete each sentence with a word from the box. Read the sentences out loud.

| fruit | chewy | few | juice |

1. We like to make _____ from our grapes.

2. You need lots of grapes, not just a _____.

3. We also make raisins, which are _____.

4. You can make lots of yummy snacks from _____.

Vowel Team /ā/: *ei, ea, eigh, ey*

The vowel sound /ā/ can be spelled with the vowel team *ei*, *ea*, *eigh*, and *ey*.

A. Look at the pictures. Say the words out loud.

1.

veil

2.

steak

3.

neighbor

4.

they

B. Read the words out loud. Circle the letters that make the /ā/ sound.

1. sleigh   **3.** great   **5.** freight

2. vein   **4.** they   **6.** prey

C. Complete each sentence with a word from the box. Read the sentences out loud.

vein	weigh	they

1. How much do you _____?

2. _____ are my neighbors.

3. The nurse had a hard time finding my _____.

Name _____ Date _____

Vowel Team /oo/: *oo*

> The vowel team *oo* can make the short *u* sound, as in the word *foot*.

A. Look at the pictures. Say the words out loud.

1.

book

2.

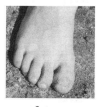

foot

3.

cookie

B. Read the words out loud. Write the words in the box.

good	room	school	took	wood
smooth	hood	gloom	brook	proof

oo as in *food*	*oo* as in *cook*

C. Finish each sentence with a word from the box.

wood	looks	good

1. My dog's house is made of _____.

2. It _____ like our own house, only it is small.

3. Dad made it. He did a very _____ job.

Vowel Team Syllables

> A syllable may contain two letters that together stand for one vowel sound. The vowel may be long, short, or a diphthong.

A. Read the examples out loud.

Long	Short	Diphthong
gain	head	loud
meat	instead	cause
piece	bread	awful
toad	book	enjoy
suit		choice

B. Put a slash between the syllables in each word. Underline the syllable that has a vowel team. Write a new word that has the same vowel team syllable on the line below.

1. painful

_____

2. employ

_____

3. bookshelf

_____

◉ **C.** Sort the words by type of underlined vowel team.

foolish
boiling
fruity
bedspread

laundry
joyful
payment
peanut

powder
cookie
headband
enjoyment

Long	Short	Diphthong

Name _____ Date _____

Chapter 5 Review

A. Complete each sentence with a word from the box below.

short	fur	first	warm	shelter
far	barked	curly	bars	birthday

1. Dad said I could have a dog. This is my _____ dog!

2. We visited the _____ to find him.

3. It is not very _____ from our home.

4. So many dogs _____ in their pens!

5. I saw one with a _____ tail, like a pig's.

6. I saw a dog with long hair and one with _____ hair.

7. I saw a dog with long, white _____.

8. I slipped my hand between the _____ of his pen.

9. This dog was soft, _____, and cuddly.

10. This dog was the perfect _____ gift!

B. Read the story out loud. If the underlined word is correct, write C. If it is wrong, write the correct word.

Would you like to <u>care</u> _____ for sick people? Are
₁₁

you not <u>scared</u> _____ of seeing big cuts? You don't
₁₂

<u>shot</u> _____ at stuff like that? <u>Good</u> _____,
₁₃ ₁₄

there's a first aid kit in your <u>purs</u> _____. Yes, the <u>pont</u>
₁₅ ₁₆

_____ is clear. You'd make a fine <u>nurs</u> _____.
₁₇

Chapter 5 Review (continued)

C. Circle the correct word to complete each sentence.

18. I went to my friend Drew's party. He is a kind (boy, boil).

19. He got lots of (town, toys) for his birthday.

20. There was a large (crown, crowd) of people there.

21. Drew's mom served (fruit, suit) for a snack.

22. Then we had Drew's favorite cake, (proud, pound) cake.

23. After cake, a (clown, brown) came to do some tricks.

24. Then we sang to Drew. He turned (sleigh, eight) that day.

25. I had such a (good, wood) time at Drew's party!

D. Read the clues. Each answer contains an *r*-controlled vowel. Complete the puzzle with words from the box.

girl   dirty   party   skirt   pork   third

Across
2. kind of meat
4. after two in line
5. not clean

Down
1. not a boy
2. a fun time
3. not pants or shorts

Syllables

Compound Words

A compound word is two words joined together to make one word. Each word is pronounced.

A. Read each pair of words out loud. Then read the compound word out loud.

1. mail box → mailbox

2. lunch box → lunchbox

3. high way → highway

4. key board → keyboard

5. earth quake → earthquake

6. sea weed → seaweed

B. Read the words out loud. Draw a slash between the two words of each compound word.

1. bookshelf

2. desktop

3. homework

4. treetop

5. fingernail

6. sunshine

7. doghouse

8. shoelace

9. sweatshirt

10. firehouse

C. Match a word from the first column to the second column to make a compound word. Many combinations are possible.

1. back   pack

2. air   ground

3. class   line

4. base   work

5. home   room

6. play   ball

Syllables

> A syllable is a word or part of a word that has only one vowel sound. For example, *rabbit* has two syllables.

A. Write the number of syllables in each word below.

1. cat _____

2. student _____

3. tiger _____

4. photograph _____

5. computer _____

6. basket _____

7. napkin _____

8. tomato _____

B. Read the words out loud. Put a slash between the syllables. Sort the words based on their syllable type.

Germany foot   reading   moment   appointment
baby   notebook   take   Friday

one syllable	two syllables	three syllables

Open Syllables: Long *a*

A syllable that ends with a vowel sound is called an open syllable. An open syllable usually has a long vowel sound, such as the long *a* sound in baby.

A. Put a slash between the syllables in these words. Then underline the open syllable with long *a*.

1. favor

2. navy

3. basis

4. radar

5. agent

6. caper

7. favorite

8. lady

B. Read each clue. Add an open syllable with *a* to complete each word.

1. a person just born   _____by

2. something you eat with eggs   _____con

3. something you write on   _____per

4. lava and ash come from this   vol_____no

5. a woman   _____dy

6. something you like more   _____vorite

Open Syllables: Long e

Remember that a syllable that ends with a vowel sound is called an **open syllable**. An open syllable usually has a long vowel sound, such as the long e sound in *prefix*.

A. Put a slash between the syllables in these words. Then underline the open syllable with long e.

1. recent

2. Peter

3. fever

4. detail

5. create

6. even

7. secret

8. legal

B. Read these sentences out loud. Underline the words with the open syllable with long e.

1. My dog is a female. That means she's a girl.

2. The ground is really hard. It's made of cement.

3. I love playing with my friends at recess.

4. Sometimes it's hard to remember to do my homework.

5. Write details about the party in your story.

6. Pam and Peter are twins.

Open Syllables: Long *i*

> Remember that a syllable that ends with a vowel sound is called an open syllable. An open syllable usually has a long vowel sound, such as the long *i* sound in *tiger*.

A. Put a slash between the syllables in the words. Then underline the open syllable with long *i*.

1. item
2. tripod
3. spider
4. digest

5. pilot
6. silent
7. vibrate
8. siren

B. Read these sentences out loud. Underline the words with the open syllable with long *i*.

1. A loud siren woke me up this morning.

2. Then a brown spider was crawling on me.

3. I jumped up and broke my mom's pretty iris.

4. I'm so glad it's Friday!

5. It's a good idea for a story.

6. The icicles hung on the trees.

Open Syllables: Long *o*

Remember that a syllable that ends with a vowel sound is called an open syllable. An open syllable usually has a long vowel sound, such as the long *o* sound in *open*.

A. Put a slash between the syllables in the words. Then underline the open syllable with long o.

1. focus

2. robot

3. notify

4. stolen

5. moment

6. polar

7. chosen

8. piano

B. Read these sentences out loud. Underline the words with the open syllable with long o.

1. I was hoping for a snow day today.

2. My friend got a cute, brown pony for her birthday.

3. I can't wait to open my birthday gifts.

4. We stayed at a motel because it was too far to drive home.

5. The travelers found an oasis in the desert.

6. We sailed across the Atlantic Ocean.

Open Syllables: Long *u*

> Remember that a syllable that ends with a vowel sound is called an open syllable. An open syllable usually has a long vowel sound, such as the long *u* sound in *music.*

A. Put a slash between the syllables in the following words. Then underline the open syllable with long *u*.

1. unit

5. human

2. duty

6. pupil

3. future

7. student

4. cubic

8. truly

B. Read these sentences out loud. Underline the words with the open syllable with long *u*.

1. Pluto was called a planet, but now it's not.

2. It was in a science unit at school.

3. I am a good student.

4. No one would ever say that I'm stupid.

5. The universe contains many solor systems.

6. The police officer's uniform is bright blue.

High Frequency Words: Set 11

A. You will see these 10 words in many books. Say the words out loud.

question	answer	listen	decision	usual
common	summary	hear	language	through

B. Read the story out loud. Circle the high frequency words in the story.

Speaking in public is a common fear, so I hear. The fear can grab you at any time. Well, it grabbed me. I had to give a summary of a film that was in the French language. I asked myself: Will anyone listen? Can I get through this? What if I can't answer any questions? I made a decision. I could not do this.

"What's up?" asked my sister Casey, and I told her.

"We have something in common," she said. "You can do that summary. I'll listen to your speech. Speak up so I can hear you."

I gave the summary. Casey listened. I answered her questions. As usual, Casey helped me. Everything was going to be fine. Then I made a decision. I could do this speech after all.

Reading Practice: Passage 11

A. Read the story out loud.

Kristin has made a decision to go to Spain to study. She is thrilled about spending a year in Spain. She will stay with a family that has two boys who will go to school with her. She will have her own room in their house so she can do her homework.

During her time in Spain, Kristin would like to learn to speak Spanish. Because she will be going to a Spanish high school, this is something that she can work on every day. Next, she would like to learn about new people. She has many questions about how Spanish people live and what they like to do. And third, she would like to take cooking lessons so she could cook good Spanish food. Then her family at home will think she's perfect!

B. Work with a partner. Answer each question.

1. What does Kristin want to learn in Spain?

2. How will she learn the Spanish language?

Home-School Connection Read the story to a family member or a friend. What language does he or she speak at home? Discuss what countries each of you would like to visit and why.

W- and *L-*influenced *a*

> The vowel *a* sometimes sounds like the vowel sound in *saw*
> when it comes after a *w* or before an *l*.

A. Read the words out loud. Circle the letter or letters that influence the *a* sound.

1. fall

2. always

3. water

4. wall

5. chalk

6. walrus

B. Read the sentences out loud. Underline the words that have the *w-* or *l-*influenced *a* sound.

1. I like to play ball games with the kids on the block.

2. Our best player is Walt. He's very tall.

3. I look up when I talk to him.

4. We all like Walt a lot.

5. After school we hang around the mall.

6. The soup needs more salt and pepper.

Syllable Stress

> In words with two or more syllables, one syllable is stressed. Hold your hand under your chin as you say a two-syllable word. Your jaw drops more for the stressed syllable.

A. Read the following words out loud as you hold your hand under your chin. Write the words in the correct column.

| away | baby | become | harvest | never |
| open | submit | suppose | survive | tender |

first syllable stressed	second syllable stressed

B. Read the story out loud. Circle the syllable that is stressed for each underlined word.

Henry is an airplane pilot. He flies a huge airplane all over
‾‾‾‾
1   2

the world, taking people to visit family and have meetings. His
              ‾‾‾‾‾
              3

airplane is purple with black stripes. Before taking off, Henry
                                        ‾‾‾‾‾‾
                                        4

makes sure everyone's seatbelts are tight. Sometimes, there is a

delay. Henry doesn't like that. Henry doesn't like that.
‾‾‾‾‾
5

Name _____   Date _____

Schwa: *a*

The letter *a* appears in the first or last syllable of many words. If that syllable is not stressed, then the sound of the *a* is a schwa. Schwa sounds like a short *u*.

A. Read these words out loud. Circle the schwa sound in each word.

1. along

2. China

3. alone

4. amuse

5. alike

6. adapt

7. about

8. ago

9. Krista

10. flora

B. Read these sentences out loud. Complete each sentence with a word from the box.

| ago | away | asleep | about | sofa | alone |

1. A while _____ I found three kittens.

2. The kittens were _____, and they were scared.

3. I carried them _____ to my house.

4. They like to play in the living room on my _____.

5. Now they are safe. They are _____ in a warm box.

6. I like to tell everyone _____ my new kittens.

Schwa: *er, or, ar*

When *er, or,* or *ar* appear in an unstressed syllable, it makes the /ur/ sound.

A. Look at the pictures. Say the words out loud. Circle the schwa sound.

1.

letter

2.

dollar

3.

doctor

4.

mother

B. Complete each sentence with a word from the box. Read the sentences out loud.

under   collar   mayor   teacher   color

1. A person who gives lessons is a _____.

2. A dog should wear a _____ around its neck.

3. The _____ runs our town.

4. My bag is _____ the desk.

5. Purple is my favorite _____.

Name _____ Date _____

Schwa: *le*

> A consonant + -*le* at the end of a word forms the last syllable. The sound you hear between the consonant and -*le* is a schwa.

A. Read the words out loud. Circle the schwa sound.

1. puzzle   **4.** battle

2. little   **5.** wobble

3. humble

B. Add -*le* to finish the words. Read the words out loud.

1. waff_____   **4.** hobb_____

2. sing_____   **5.** freck_____

3. purp_____

C. Complete each sentence with a word from the box.

bottle   middle   uncle

1. Today is the first day of _____ school.

2. My aunt and _____ will drive me.

3. I have a _____ of water to drink.

CVCle Syllables

A consonant + -*le* at the end of a word forms the last syllable. If the first syllable ends in a consonant, it has a short vowel. If it ends in a vowel, the syllable has a long vowel sound.

A. Read the words out loud. Circle the short vowel sounds and underline the long vowel sounds.

1. han/dle

4. ta/ble

2. bot/tle

5. bu/gle

3. un/cle

B. Put a slash between the syllables in these words. Underline the CVCle syllable. Write short or long to tell about the first syllable.

1. simple _____

3. needle _____

2. tumble _____

4. bridle _____

C. Read the rhyme aloud. Underline the words that contain a CVCle syllable.

There's a puzzle on the table.
Solve it if you think you're able.
We can solve it in the stable.

High Frequency Words: Set 12

A. You will see these 10 words in many books. Say the words out loud.

once	special	character	sure	thought
although	vocabulary	culture	beautiful	way

B. Read the story out loud. Underline the high frequency words in the story.

Each culture has its own way of telling tales. In every story, the main character has a problem. We learn about his or her thoughts and feelings through what they do and say. Although the character has problems, we know he or she will be happy in the end.

There is special storytelling vocabulary for reading aloud these beautiful tales. A sentence that begins "Once upon a time" is a sure way of starting a story. These words mean a beautiful tale is about to start. A sentence that says "happily ever after" is a sure way of ending a story. These words mean the beautiful tale is over.

What is some storytelling vocabulary of your culture? What are your thoughts about his vocabulary?

Reading Practice: Passage 12

A. Read the story out loud.

A baby bird grows inside an egg. Its beak is very soft. So how does the baby bird get out of the egg? The baby bird has an egg tooth. This special tooth helps the baby bird peck its way out of the shell.

A single egg tooth grows at the end of the bird's little beak. It is quite small, but it's very hard. The baby bird taps the egg tooth on the inside of the shell until it breaks open. Then the baby bird can wobble out of the shell. Later on, the baby bird will be a little more stable. He will ruffle his feathers and walk around. The special egg tooth that helped him get out of his shell will fall off.

B. Work with a partner. Answer each question.

1. What does an egg tooth do?

2. What happens to the egg tooth after the baby bird is more stable?

Home-School Connection Read the story to a family member or a friend. Have either of you seen a baby bird come out its shell? If so, describe what it was like.

Name _____   Date _____

Chapter 6 Review

A. Circle the correct word to complete each sentence.

1. With much (protest, pretty), I had to go to the dentist.

2. I do not like the dentist, but I do not want to act like a (babby, baby).

3. In fact, I was truly (beeside, beside) myself.

4. At the moment, I was (frozen, frozzen) with fright.

5. I heard (footsteps, footballs) coming down the hall.

6. Then I saw her. It was a (female, femmale) dentist.

7. She put out her hand to give me a (handball, handshake).

8. I used her (barefoot, footstool) to get into the chair.

9. She put on some soft (mussic, music) for me to listen to.

10. It wasn't so bad. I even got a new (toothbrush, hairbrush)!

B. Read the story out loud. Fix the spelling of the underlined words. If the word is correct, write C.

Bess and Jill went to the <u>mawl</u> _____ for a new dress.
11

Bess is very <u>taull</u> _____, so she had to try each dress on. They
12

<u>walked</u> _____ around for hours and drank a bottle of <u>watter</u>
13   14

_____. Then they <u>cawlled</u> _____ Bess's mom to pick
15

them up. Those girls <u>allways</u> _____ have a <u>ball</u> _____ at
16   17

the mall!

Chapter 6 Review (continued)

C. Circle the correct word to complete each sentence.

18. My Gramps is a foot (doctor, docter).

19. Grams is the (mayer, mayor) of our town.

20. They have saved many (dollers, dollars) so they can retire.

21. Grams wants to ride her bike (around/eround) the world.

22. My mom has a (better/bettur) thought.

23. She wants them to (settle/settel) down and relax.

24. They can (sampel, sample) fine wines.

25. They can enjoy some quiet time (alone, ulone).

26. They can do crossword (puzzels/puzzles) on the couch.

27. Grams and Gramps (grumbeled, grumbled). They still want to work.

D. Read each clue. Unscramble the syllables and write each word. Then put a slash to separate the syllables and underline the open syllable.

28. a student   pilpu _____

29. a notebook has this   perpa _____

30. not a father   thermo _____

31. not loud   lentsi _____

32. Thanksgiving time   Nobervem _____

Complex Consonants

Soft c

The letter *c* can have a soft sound when it comes before *e*, *i*, or *y*, for example, *city*.

A. Read the words out loud. Circle the soft *c* sound.

1. race   **2.** circus   **3.** rice   **4.** cell   **5.** icy

B. Read the grocery list out loud. Underline the words that contain soft *c*.

Things to buy:

celery   rice
carrots   cake
ice cream   citrus fruits
chicken   spices

C. Complete each sentence with a word from the box.

citizen   center   citrus   circle

1. Please place the flowers in the _____ of the table.

2. We sat in a _____ to play the game.

3. I am a _____ of the United States.

4. Lemons are _____ fruits.

Soft *c* and Hard *c*

> Remember that the letter *c* can have a soft sound, as in *city*.
> It can also have a hard sound when it comes before *a, o,* or *u,*
> for example, *cat*.

A. Read the words out loud. Circle the hard *c* sound.

1. carrot

5. coat

2. cot

6. cave

3. cut

7. corn

4. cable

8. comb

B. Read the words in the box out loud. Write the words in the
   correct column.

mice	fancy	cent	cell	call	city	case
cease	cute	cite	cost	count	cone	cane

hard *c*	soft *c*

Soft *g*

The letter *g* can have a soft sound when it comes before *e*, *i*, or *y*, for example, *geometry*.

A. Read the words out loud. Circle the soft *g* sound.

1. germ   **2.** gem   **3.** ginger   **4.** gentle

B. Read the sentences out loud. Underline the words that contain soft *g*, as in *gem*.

1. Today in class, Mr. Gentry decided to teach us a German dance.

2. My partner was Gerry.

3. We danced in the gym.

4. I held Gerry's hand gently.

5. Mr. Gentry told us to act like ladies and gentlemen.

C. Complete each sentence with a word from the box.

strange	cage	magic

1. Yesterday we saw a _____ show.

2. I saw a white bird in a _____.

3. Suddenly it disappeared. How _____!

Name _____ Date _____

Soft *g*: *-ge* and *-dge*

> The letters *-ge* and *-dge* at the the end of a word stand for the soft *g* sound.

A. Read the words out loud. Circle the soft *g* sound.

1. bridge   **2.** ledge   **3.** huge   **4.** fudge   **5.** rage

B. Read the clues. Add *-ge* or *-dge* to complete the answers. Then read the words out loud.

1. This helps you cross over a river.   bri_____

2. This means "very big."   hu_____

3. Your book has a lot of these.   pa_____

4. This person tells which is the best.   ju_____

5. You perform a play here.   sta_____

C. Complete each sentence with a word from the box.

fudge   judge   huge

1. There was a _____ contest at the fair.

2. Who made the best sweet _____?

3. Each _____ tasted the chocolate treats.

Soft *g* and Hard *g*

> Remember that the letter *g* can have a soft sound. It can also have a hard sound when it comes before *a*, *o*, or *u*, for example, *go*.

A. Read the words out loud. Circle the hard *g* sound.

1. gate   **2.** goat   **3.** gold   **4.** gum   **5.** ginger

B. Read the words out loud. List the words in the correct column on the chart.

goal	age	dodge	gentle	gone
get	magic	germ	goat	gust

hard *g*	soft *g*

C. Complete each sentence with a word from the box.

gave	gold	golf

1. _____ is a fun sport.

2. My dad _____ me a set of golf clubs.

3. The clubs came in a bright _____ bag.

Final -ve

Usually, words with the pattern CVCe have a long vowel sound, as in *home*. Sometimes, when *-ve* is at the end of a word or syllable, the vowel sound is short.

A. Read the words out loud. Circle the short vowel sound.

1. give   **2.** have   **3.** love   **4.** dove   **5.** brave

B. The following words end in -ve. Some have a short vowel sound, but some have a long vowel sound. Underline the words that have a short vowel sound and circle the words that have a long vowel sound.

gave   grove
have   hive
love   Dave
stove   cave
glove   give

C. Complete each sentence with a word from the box.

live   dove   have   glove

1. The _____ is the bird of peace.

2. A _____ will keep your hand warm.

3. I _____ in a small house.

4. I _____ a dog and three fish as pets.

Name _____ Date _____

Initial and Final *ph*

Digraphs are two letters that make one sound. The digraph *ph* makes the *f* sound.

A. Read the words out loud. Circle the *f* sound.

1.

phone

2.

photograph

3.

graph

B. Read each sentence out loud. Circle the word or words that have the *f* sound, spelled with *ph*.

1. Mrs. Philips likes teaching phonics to first graders.

2. Physical education is my favorite subject in school.

3. Phoebe and Paul like to talk on the phone.

4. We took this photograph of my family on vacation.

C. Read this ad. Circle the correct words.

It's back to school time!
Get your child's (photo, foto) taken.
We can do it (phast, fast)!
Come down now for a (phree, free) photo!

Name _____   Date _____

Initial *wr*

> The *r* sound can be spelled with *wr*. The *w* is silent.

A. Read the *wr* words out loud. Circle the *r* sound.

1.

wrench

2.

wrist

3.

wreath

B. Read the words in the box out loud. Circle them in the word find.

| write | wrong | wrap | wring | wrist | wrote | wreck |

i	w	d	e	r	c	w
w	r	i	t	e	o	r
r	i	e	d	u	e	i
o	n	l	c	t	l	s
n	g	o	o	t	a	t
g	o	r	l	a	r	n
e	w	r	e	c	k	h
w	r	a	p	d	a	d

Initial *kn*

> The *n* sound can be spelled with *kn*. The *k* is silent.

A. Read the words out loud. Circle the *n* sound.

1.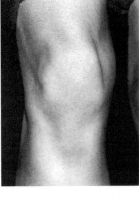

knee

2.

knife

3.

knot

B. Complete each sentence with a word from the box.

knows	knit	knock	knife	knot	knee

1. Can you _____ a warm, pretty scarf for the winter?

2. My grandmother _____ how.

3. I like to sit by her _____ and help her.

4. The cat likes to _____ over her knitting bag to play with the yarn.

5. When she gets to the end, Granny ties a small

_____ .

6. She uses scissors, not a _____ to cut the yarn.

Initial and Final *gn*

> The *n* sound can be spelled with *gn*. The *g* is silent.

A. Read the words out loud. Circle the *n* sound.

1.

gnome

2.

sign

3.

gnu

B. Read each sentence out loud. Circle the word or words that have the *n* sound, spelled with *gn*.

1. I will sign up for English as a Foreign Language classes.

2. Look at that sign. It tells about a contest at school.

3. I will design a poster for school.

4. A gnat is a small insect that gnaws.

5. Will Miss Jones assign us a lot of homework?

C. Complete the rhyme with a *gn* word.

There once was a small fly, a _____,
Who buzzed around, biting my cat.
The cat rolled over,
And that was the end of the _____.

Name _____ Date _____

Final *mb* and *bt*

> Sometimes two letters at the end of a word make one sound.
> The letters *mb* at the end of a word make the *m* sound. The
> letters *bt* at the end of a word make the *t* sound. The *b* is
> silent.

A. Read the words out loud. Circle the silent *b*.

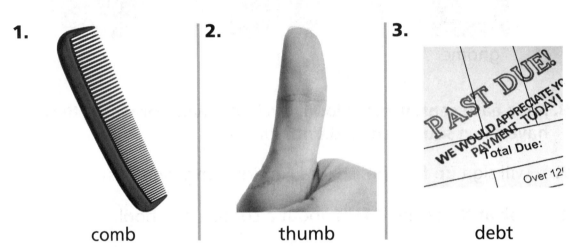

1.	2.	3.
comb	thumb	debt

B. Read each sentence out loud. Circle the word that has a
silent *b*.

1. Mom lent me money. I will pay my debt when I get paid.

2. I ate all of my sandwich. Not a crumb is left.

3. I comb my hair before going to school.

4. I will try to climb up that hill.

5. A baby sheep is called a lamb.

6. The limb of the tree was broken.

7. I doubt that we will go to the zoo tomorrow.

Reading Practice: Passage 13

A. Read the story out loud.

> This summer I am volunteering at the animal shelter near my home. I do odd jobs like answer the phones and write letters. I also help dogs get adopted. I play with them and walk them. This makes the dogs happy. A happy dog is more likely to be gentle when people come to the door of the cage.
>
> Sometimes I get attached to a dog. That's what happened with Max, a sheepdog who is as gentle as a lamb. We became instant buddies. Max would let me comb his fur and take out the knots. Then one day a family came in and fell in love with him. Just like that, they took him home. I was happy for Max, but sad for me. I am still glad I decided to volunteer at the animal shelter.

B. Work with a partner. Answer each question.

1. What did he do at the animal center?

2. Where did Max go?

Read the story to a family or a friend. Talk about how you felt when Max found a new home. Have either of you adopted a pet from a shelter? Describe the experience.

Silent *h*

> The *h* in some words is silent.

A. Read the words out loud. Circle the silent *h*.

1.

mechanic

2.

herbs

3.

hour

4.

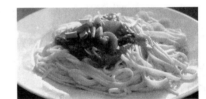

spaghetti

B. Read the clues. Unscramble the letters and write the word. The answers contain silent *h*. Then read the words out loud.

1. twenty-four in a day   urohs _____

2. plants that you use for cooking   berhs _____

3. someone who works on cars   hnemcaci _____

4. something you eat for dinner   gphtesati _____

5. someone who tells the truth   noshet _____

6. great respect   rhoon _____

Silent *l*

L is silent in some words.

A. Read the words out loud. Circle the silent *l*.

1.

yolk

2.

salmon

3.

chalk

4.

folks

B. Complete each sentence with a word from the box.

yolk	walk	salmon	stalks	chalk	talk

1. The yellow part of an egg is the _____.

2. Can your baby sister _____ yet?

3. The fish I like best is _____.

4. The teacher writes with _____ on the blackboard.

5. My sister loves to _____ on the phone.

6. Corn grows on _____.

Silent *p* and *s*

P is silent before *n*, *s*, or *t*, and sometimes before *b*. *S* can also be silent in some words.

A. Read the words out loud. Circle the silent *p* and *s*.

1.	**2.**

island	cupboard
3.	**4.**

raspberry	debris

B. Read the clues. Unscramble the letters and write the words. Circle the silent *p* or *s*. Then read the words out loud.

1. land in the middle of water   dlansi _____

2. a black or red berry   yprasrrbe _____

3. trash   ersdbi _____

4. shelf to keep dishes   bpcuoadr _____

5. proof of purchase   perteic _____

Name _____ Date _____

Silent *t*

T is silent in some words, especially in words that end in *-et,* *-ot,* or *-ut.*

A. Read the words out loud. Circle the silent *t.*

1.

ballet

2.

listen

3.

buffet

4.

castle

B. Read the clues. Unscramble the letters and write the words.
The answers contain silent *t.* Then read the words out loud.

1. a big old house in fairy tales   talcse _____

2. to hear   teslin _____

3. dance done on toes   lalbet _____

4. food and drinks at a long table   teffub _____

5. to make soft   fotens _____

Initial *gu*

The letters *gu* often make the sound *g*. The *u* is silent.

A. Read the words out loud. Circle the *g* sound.

1.  guard	**2.**  guest
3.  guitar	**4.**  guide

B. Read the words out loud. Circle them in the word find.

guarantee	guide	guilt	guitar	guest

m   t   g   u   i   t   a   r   b

g   u   a   r   a   n   t   e   e

u   a   i   a   s   o   r   g   t

i   c   u   l   h   a   u   u   y

d   k   o   o   t   l   i   i   c

e   q   h   i   e   a   t   l   m

p   g   u   e   s   t   n   t   n

a   n   e   i   r   t   h   u   c

x   i   e   w   z   a   r   i   r

Silent *w*

In some words, especially those containing *wh*, the *w* is silent.

A. Read the words out loud. Circle the silent *w*.

1. whole   **5.** two

2. sword   **6.** wrong

3. answer   **7.** write

4. whose   **8.** toward

B. Answer with a word that contains silent *w*. Put the underlined letters together to get the answer to the puzzle.

1. to respond   □□□□□□

2. to put pen on paper   □□□□□

3. two halves   □□□□□

4. incorrect   □□□□□

5. to move close to   □□□□□□

The pen is mightier than the □□□□□!

Reading Practice: Passage 14

A. Read the story out loud.

Did you ever think of the many parts of a plant you can eat? There's the root, stem, leaves, and fruit. Don't forget the seeds!

Did you know that turnips and radishes are roots? So are potatoes. If you've eaten celery or asparagus, you've eaten a stem. Spinach is a green leaf, and an apple is a red fruit. Do you like pumpkin seeds and sunflower seeds? Think about what plant part is in a glass of fruit juice. Although it's mostly water, juice comes from the fruit of the plant.

What did you eat for lunch? Was it a root, stem, leaf, or fruit? Eating some of each part of a plant each day will help you stay healthy and strong.

B. Work with a partner. Answer each question.

1. Which parts of a plant do we eat?

2. Which plant part is in a glass of juice?

Home-School Connection Read the story to a family member or a friend. Talk about your favorites fruits or vegetables. Do you both like the same ones?

Name _____ Date _____

Chapter 7 Review

A. Complete each sentence with a word from the box below.

stage	forced	strange	ballet	island
grocery	ice	cob	rice	listen

1. What if you were stranded on an _____?

2. There would be no _____ store.

3. You would not eat strawberry _____ cream.

4. You would not eat _____ and beans.

5. You would not eat corn on the _____.

6. You'd be _____ to eat coconuts all day.

7. You'd eat lots of _____ things, I bet.

8. You could dance _____ if you wanted to.

9. You could sing and nobody would _____.

10. The whole island could be your _____.

B. Read the paragraph out loud. Fix the spelling of the underlined words. If it is correct, write C.

Would you like to study in <u>Gurmany</u> _____? Many

11

<u>exchang</u> _____ programs offer you that <u>chans</u>

12   13

_____. <u>Lisen</u> _____ to how people speak the

              14

<u>languag</u> _____. You will feel <u>calm</u> _____. You

15   16

will <u>anser</u> _____ when people speak to you.

   17

Chapter 7 Review (continued)

C. Circle the correct word to complete each sentence.

18. I have two pet (mis/mice).

19. Pinky has a pink (fas/face).

20. They live in a fancy (cage/caje).

21. I keep them in a sunny (plas/place).

22. I have had them (since/sinc) August.

23. They like to (ras/race) on their wheels.

24. They love to (gnaw/naw) on things.

25. Their space is littered with (debris/debree).

26. I (change/chang) the bedding every week.

27. When their place is clean, they (danse/dance) and squeal.

D. Read the clues. Write the correct word from the box.

fudge	knife	phone	hour	wrong

28. not right   _____

29. you call someone on this   _____

30. sweet, yummy treat   _____

31. you cut with this   _____

32. sixty minutes   _____

CHAPTER 8

Prefixes and Suffixes

Prefixes: *dis-, un-*

When *dis-* or *un-* is added to a base word, the new word means the opposite of the base word.

Base Word	Prefixes: *dis-/un-*
agree	disagree
appear	disappear
comfort	discomfort
happy	unhappy
baked	unbaked
lock	unlock

Add *dis-* or *un-* to the word in parentheses. Use a dictionary if you need to. Write the new word on the line.

1. (lock) Will you help me _____ this window?

2. (like) I _____ the smell of garlic.

3. (true) That story is simply _____.

4. (obey) You should not _____ your teacher.

5. (infect) We must _____ the cut on your finger.

6. (explored) Much of Alaska is _____.

7. (cooked) Eating _____ eggs can make you sick.

8. (wrap) I want to _____ my gifts now.

Name _____ Date _____

Prefixes: *over-*, *re-*

The prefix *over-* means "too much" or "higher." The prefix *re-* means "again." For example, *overeat* means "to eat too much," and *revisit* means "to visit again."

A. Add *over-* or *re-* to the word. Use a dictionary if you need to. Write the new word on the line.

1. flow _____ **4.** tell _____

2. grown _____ **5.** glue _____

3. paint _____ **6.** seal _____

B. Add *over-* or *re-* to the words in the box. Then choose a word to complete each sentence. Write the word on the line.

_____seas	_____play	_____phrase
_____due	_____sized	

1. The books should have been returned to the library. They are
   _____.

2. My brother traveled across the Atlantic. He went
   _____.

3. This bed is bigger than normal. It is _____.

4. Please say that again. _____ it in simpler language.

5. I love to listen to that song. Will you _____ it for me?

Prefix: *non-*

When *non-* is added to a base word, the new word means the opposite of the base word. For example, *nonsense* means "doesn't make sense."

A. Add *non-* to the words. Write the new word on the line.

1. profit   _____

2. stop   _____

3. fat   _____

4. fiction   _____

5. verbal   _____

B. Add *non-* to the words in the box. Then choose a word to answer each clue. Write the word on the line.

_____dairy	_____living	_____smoker
_____stick	_____toxic	_____verbal

1. safe to eat   _____

2. doesn't stick   _____

3. not alive   _____

4. someone who doesn't smoke   _____

5. doesn't eat milk or cheese   _____

6. doesn't use spoken language   _____

Name _____   Date _____

Prefixes: *uni-*, *bi-*, *tri-*

The prefixes *uni-* means "one" or "the same," *bi-* means "two," and *tri-* means "three." For example, *unicycle* means "one-wheeled cycle," *biannual* means "happening twice a year," and *triangle* means "a shape with three sides and angles."

A. Read the clues. Add the correct prefix to complete the words. Use a dictionary if you need to.

1. 200 years after an important event   _____ centennial

2. having three colors   _____ color

3. glasses with two lenses   _____ focals

4. a stand with three legs   _____ pod

5. going in only one direction   _____ directional

B. Finish the words in the box using *uni-*, *bi-*, or *tri-*. Then use the words to complete the sentences.

_____ form   _____ cycle   _____ monthly   _____ lingual

1. We meet two times a month. It's a _____ meeting.

2. My sister is only two. She still needs to ride a _____.

3. Students at our school dress the same. They must wear a

_____.

4. Jose can speak three languages. He's _____.

Suffixes: *-ness*, *-ful*

> The suffix *-ness* means "the quality of being." It changes an adjective into a noun. The suffix *-ful* means "full of." It changes a noun into an adjective. If the base word ends in *y*, change the *y* to *i* before adding *-ness* or *-ful*. For example, *happy* becomes *happiness*; *beauty* becomes *beautiful*.

A. Add *-ness* or *-ful* to the word in parentheses to complete each sentence.

1. The peach was very (flavor) _____.

2. The student's (weak) _____ is in math.

3. The (empty) _____ made the room look big.

4. The lunch is filled with wholesome (good) _____.

5. Apples are (plenty) _____ in the fall.

B. Read the story. Fix the spelling of the underlined words. If the spelling is correct, write C.

Mom made me a new shirt. The fabric is so bright and <u>colorfull</u>
₁

_____. It really is a <u>beautyful</u> _____ shirt.
₂

It has one <u>weakness</u> _____, though. Mom forgot to
₃

put buttons on it. I have to be very careful when putting it on.

I don't want to rip it. Mom can be so <u>forgetfull</u> _____!
₄

Suffixes: -*ly*, -*al*

The suffix -*ly* means "in a certain way." It changes an adjective into an adverb. The suffix -*al* means "like" or "of." It changes a noun into an adjective. If the base word ends in *y*, change the *y* to *i* before adding -*ly*. For example, *angry* becomes *angrily*. Sometimes you must drop the *e* when adding -*al*. For example, *arrive* becomes *arrival*.

A. Add -*ly* or -*al* to the word in parentheses. Write the new word on the line. Read the sentences out loud.

1. (nature)   This fruit bar is made with all _____ flavors.

2. (arrive)   We were all there for Mom's _____.

3. (hungry)   The stray dog ate _____.

4. (quick)   We must finish our chores _____.

5. (logic)   Your thinking is not _____.

B. Read the clues. Unscramble the letters. The answers contain the suffix -*ly* or -*al*. Write the words on the lines.

1. not quickly   lyslow _____

2. having to do with industries   ridusintal _____

3. the least possible amount   alnimim _____

4. in a gentle way   lygent _____

5. having logic   icallog _____

Name _____ Date _____

Suffixes: *-ment, -less*

The suffix *-ment* shows an action or state. It changes a
verb into a noun. If the base word ends in *y*, change the
y to *i* before adding *-ment*. For example, *merry* becomes
merriment. The suffix *-less* means "without." *Hopeless* means
"without hope."

**A. Add *-ment* or *-less* to the word in parentheses. Write the new
word on the line. Read the sentences out loud.**

1. (amuse)   We went to an _____ park on Sunday.

2. (develop)   The new housing _____ went up quickly.

3. (pain)   The doctor gave me a shot so the surgery was

                    _____.

4. (care)   The student made _____ mistakes on
his test.

5. (amaze)   I watched in _____ as the dog played
with the cat.

6. (end)   The movie was so long. It was _____.

B. Add *-ment* or *-less* to the words. Read the words out loud.

1. taste _____   4. ship _____

2. end _____   5. govern _____

3. help _____   6. age _____

Suffixes: *-or*, *-ist*

> The suffixes *-or* and *-ist* mean "one who." For example, an *actor* is "one who acts." A *novelist* is "one who writes."

A. Add *-ist* or *-or* to the word in parentheses. Write the new word on the line.

1. (motor) The _____ crashed his car into the wall.

2. (invent) Alexander Bell is the _____ of the phone.

3. (drug) The _____ gave me medicine so I will feel better.

4. (collect) Sally is a stamp _____.

5. (final) I am a _____ in the State Drawing Contest.

B. Read the story below. Fix the spelling of the underlined words. If the word is correct, write C.

What should I be when I grow up? I like to draw, so

maybe I'll become an <u>artisst</u> _____ or a <u>sculpter</u>
        1   2

_____. I always make sure that my teeth are clean,

so maybe I'll be a <u>dentist</u> _____. I also like to
        3

write, so I could be an <u>authur</u> _____ or <u>novelist</u>
        4   5

_____. Whatever I become, I'll do a great job!

Suffix: -ous

The suffix -ous means "having the quality of." It changes a noun into an adjective. The word *famous* means "having the quality of fame." Sometimes you must drop the e when adding -ous. For example, *fame* becomes *famous*.

A. Read the clues. Unscramble the letters. The answers contain the suffix -ous. Read the words out loud.

1. not safe   ousdanerg _____

2. not relaxed, upset   noervus _____

3. very funny   orhumous _____

4. very brave   corugaoeus _____

B. Add -ous to the words in the box. Finish each sentence with one of the words. Then read the sentences out loud.

hazard_____	poison_____	joy_____	adventur_____

1. The black widow spider is _____. One bite can kill a small animal.

2. Paul loves traveling to far away places. He's really
   _____.

3. Sara was so happy when she scored the goal. She let out a
   _____ scream.

4. Those chemicals are unsafe to be around. They are
   _____.

Name _____ Date _____

Suffixes: *-tion*, *-sion*

The suffixes *-tion* and *-sion* change verbs into nouns. When the base word ends in *-t*, use *-tion*. When the base word ends in *-ss*, use -sion. Note spelling changes.

Base Word	Suffixes: *-tion/-sion*
pollute	pollution
perfect	perfection
possess	possession
impress	impression

Add *-tion* or *-sion* to the word in parentheses. Write the new word on the line. Read the sentences out loud.

1. (profess)   Teaching is an important _____.

2. (discuss)   We had a long _____ about math grades.

3. (imitate)   I can do a good _____ of Elvis.

4. (instruct)   Please find the _____ manual and read it to me.

5. (promote)   Dad got a well-deserved _____ at work.

6. (adopt)   The _____ process will take two years.

7. (impress)   Always try to make a good first _____.

8. (pollute)   _____ is bad for the environment.

Suffixes: *-able, -ible*

> The suffixes *-able* and *-ible* mean "can be done." Add *-able* to base words. Add *-ible* to roots. Sometimes there are exceptions, such as *response* and *responsible*.

Root/Base Word	Suffixes: *-ible/-able*
vis	visible
poss	possible
terr	terrible
understand	understandable
comfort	comfortable
enjoy	enjoyable

A. Add *-able* or *-ible* to the word in parentheses. Write the new word on the line. Read the sentences out loud.

1. (afford)   My dad purchased a small, _____ car.

2. (wash)   The dress is _____ in cold water.

3. (depend)   Our car is old, but at least it's _____.

B. Add *-able* or *-ible* to complete each word.

It's imposs_____ to go anywhere with my four-year-old
            1

brother. He can't be near anything break_____. It's not that he's
                                          2

irrespons_____. Mom says his behavior is understand_____.
         3   4

Still, when something breaks, I wish I were invis_____.
                                                  5

Reading Practice: Passage 15

A. Read the story below.

Ray was bored. In the middle of winter vacation, both of his best buddies were out of town. Jake was visiting his grandmother in Illinois. Tom was on an expedition in Alaska. Unhappily, Ray stared out the window at the new snow. Right now, they would all be having a snowball fight, if only they were in the same location.

Feeling hopeless, Ray decided to go exploring outside. Everything was silent after the snowfall. He walked up the block, past Jake's house and Tom's house. Then he saw someone ahead, busily rolling a ball of snow in a front yard. It was a boy about his age. Ray went over for an introduction.

The boy smiled and said, "Hey, I'm Steve. I'm visiting from Oregon. This snow is awesome. Do you want to help me make a fort?" Ray decided that today would be a great occasion to build a fort with a new friend.

B. Work with a partner. Answer each question.

1. Why is Ray bored?

2. What does Ray decide to do after he meets Steve?

Home-School Connection Read the story to a family member or a friend. Talk about a time you made a new friend.

Name _____ Date _____

Chapter 8 Review

A. Add the prefix *dis-*, *un-*, *re-*, or *over-* to the word in parentheses. Write the new word on the line.

1. Mom was (happy) _____ with my math grade.

2. She wants me to (take) _____ the test tomorrow.

3. I don't want Mom to (react) _____.

4. But I don't want to (obey) _____ her.

5. My teacher was (joyed) _____ to help me.

6. "Here's your test," she said. "(view) _____ it."

7. I saw that I had (looked) _____ the other side!

8. "Your test is (finished) _____," said my teacher.

9. "Your bad grade can (appear) _____!"

10. Wow! A second chance! This is (expected) _____!

B. Read the paragraph below. Fix the spelling mistakes in the underlined words. If it is correct, write C.

Homeschooling is the <u>educasion</u> _____ of children at

home. Homeschooling is an <u>opsion</u> _____ for parents
11   12

who need a <u>flexable</u> _____ schedule. Homeschooling
13

may also involve <u>instructsion</u> _____ under the <u>supervition</u>
14   15

_____ of a formal school. Often, homeschooling

parents have <u>discussions</u> _____ to plan for the <u>fuchur</u>
16   17

_____.

Chapter 8 Review (continued)

C. Circle the correct word to complete each sentence.

18. At my house, everyone is (responsable/responsible) for the chores.

19. When the grass is (ungrown/overgrown), I cut it.

20. When paint on the house is chipping, Dad (repaints/nonpaints) it.

21. Lynn uses a (nonstick/unstick) pan to make breakfast.

22. We have a garden, so vegetables are (plentyful/plentiful).

23. My favorites are the (colorful/colorfull) bell peppers.

24. Our apples signal the (arriveal/arrival) of fall.

25. We harvest the fruits and vegetables (quickly/quickful).

26. We conserve the (goodness/goodfull) by drying the fruit.

27. These snacks are delicious and (inexpensive/inexpenseful).

D. Read each clue. Unscramble the syllables to find the answer. Write each word. Underline each suffix.

28. to assist   lhpfelu _____

29. without value   setwrohsl _____

30. plays the piano   istanpi _____

31. very large or great mendoustre _____

32. one who inspects   specintor _____

Consonant Reminders

Consonant Sound-Spellings	
/b/ spelled *b*	**b**ird
/d/ spelled *d*	**d**ollar
/f/ spelled *f, ph*	**f**arm, **ph**one
/g/ spelled *g*	**g**olf
/h/ spelled *h*	**h**ead
/j/ spelled *j, g, dge*	**j**oke, **g**erm, **g**iraffe, **g**ym, bri**dge**
/k/ spelled *c, ck, k*	**c**omputer, ro**ck**et, **k**itten
/l/ spelled *l*	**l**emon
/m/ spelled *m*	**m**ath
/n/ spelled *n, kn, gn*	**n**urse, **kn**ees, si**gn**
/p/ spelled *p*	**p**encil
/r/ spelled *r, wr*	**r**ight, **wr**ong
/s/ spelled *s, c*	**s**andwich, **c**enter, **c**ircle, **c**ycle
/t/ spelled *t*	**t**ime
/v/ spelled *v*	**v**isit
/w/ spelled *w, wh*	**w**orld, **wh**at
/y/ spelled *y*	**y**oung
/z/ spelled *z, s*	**z**one, ro**s**e

Consonant Digraphs	
/ch/ spelled *ch, tch*	**ch**ildren, i**tch**
/sh/ spelled *sh*	**sh**oe
/th/ spelled *th*	**th**ank (unvoiced), **th**ey (voiced)
/hw/ spelled *wh*	**wh**y

Consonant Generalizations

When two of the same consonants appear side-by-side in a word, only one is heard: *drummer*

When the letter *c* is followed by the vowels *o* or *a*, the *c* stands for the /k/ sound: *cat, cotton*

When the letter *c* is followed by the letters *e*, *i*, or *y*, the *c* stands for the /s/ sound: *cent, city, cycle*

When the letter *g* is followed by the letters *i*, *e*, or *y*, the *g* usually stands for the /j/ sound: *gentle, giant, gym*

Vowel Reminders

Short Vowel Sound-Spellings

/a/ spelled *a*	chat
/e/ spelled *e*	neck
/i/ spelled *i*	list
/o/ spelled *o*	clock
/u/ spelled *u*	luck

Long Vowel Sound-Spellings

/ā/ spelled *a_e, ay, ai*	brave, stay, wait
/ē/ spelled *ee, ea, e, ie, ey, y*	agree, jeans, she, puppies, key, silly
/ī/ spelled *i_e, igh, ie, i, y*	dime, light, tries, wild, why
/ō/ spelled *o_e, oa, ow, o, oe*	note, throat, known, cold, toe
/ū/ spelled *u_e, u, oo, ew, ui, oe*	cute, human, moon, few, fruit, shoe

Dipthong Sound-Spellings

/ou/ spelled *ou, ow*	house, crowded
/aw/ spelled *aw, au*	lawn, cause
/oi/ spelled *oi, oy*	coin, enjoy
/oo/ spelled *oo*	foot

R-Controlled Vowel Sound-Spellings

/är/ spelled *ar*	party
/ôr/ spelled *or, ore, our*	sports, more, four
/ûr/ spelled *er, ir, ur, ear, or, ar*	serve, birthday, Thursday, learn, work, calendar
/âr/ spelled *air, are*	chair, square

Vowel Generalizations

When a word has only one vowel letter, the vowel sound is usually short: *cub*

The vowel *a* is influenced by *w* and *l*, and can make the /aw/ sound: *wall*

If there is one vowel letter in an accented syllable, the vowel has a short sound: *little*

When a word has a VCe pattern, the first vowel is usually long: *rope*

If a vowel is at the end of a syllable, the vowel is long: *me*

Two vowels can represent a single, long vowel sound: *sea*

When a vowel is followed by *r*, that vowel is neither long nor short, but *r*-controlled: *car*

Two vowels can make two separate sounds that are said as one sound: *house*

The vowel in an unaccented syllable usually makes the schwa sound: *sofa*

Syllable Reminders

There are six types of syllables:	
1. *Closed*: CVC, CCVC, CVCC, CCVCC	cat, stop, milk, spend
2. *Open*: CV, CCV	**pi**lot, **stu**dent
3. *Vowel-Silent* e: CVCe, CCVCe, CVCCe	wh**ale**, br**oke**, p**aste**
4. *Vowel Team*: CVVC, CCVVC, CVVCC	t**ea**m, pr**oo**f, f**au**lt
5. *R-Controlled*: CVrC, CCVrC, CVrCC	sh**or**t, sm**ar**t,
6. *Consonant*-le: Cle, CCle	pu**zzle**, ge**ntle**

Syllable Generalizations

In a word with two or more syllables, one syllable receives more stress.

Inflectional endings such as *-ed*, *-ing*, *-ies*, prefixes, and suffixes often form separate syllables.

If the first vowel sound in a word is followed by two consonants, the first syllable usually ends with the first of the two consonants: *rib bon*

If the first vowel sound in a word is followed by a single consonant, that consonant usually begins the second syllable: *pa per*

In most two-syllable nouns, the first syllable is stressed: *pen'cil, dog'house, fe'male*

When a two-syllable word ends with a consonant and a *y*, the first syllable is usually stressed and the last syllable is usually unstressed: *pup'py*